CW00410418

Theological Foundations
for
New Covenant Ethics

A. Blake White

Other Books by A. Blake White:

The Newness of the New Covenant
The Law of Christ: A Theological Proposal
Galatians: A Theological Interpretation
Abide in Him: A Theological Interpretation of
John's First Letter
Union with Christ: Last Adam & Seed of Abraham
What is New Covenant Theology? An Introduction

Theological Foundations
for
New Covenant Ethics

A. Blake White

5317 Wye Creek Drive, Frederick, MD 21703-6938
301-473-8781 | info@newcovenantmedia.com
www.NewCovenantMedia.com

Theological Foundations for New Covenant Ethics

Copyright 2013© by A. Blake White.

Published by: New Covenant Media
                    5317 Wye Creek Drive
                    Frederick, Maryland 21703-6938

Orders: www.newcovenantmedia.com

Cover design by Matthew Tolbert.

All rights reserved. No part of this publication may be reproduced, stored in a retrieval system, or transmitted in any form by any means, electronic, mechanical, photocopy, recording, or otherwise without the prior permission of the publisher, except as provided by USA copyright law.

Printed in the United States of America

ISBN 13: 978-1-928965-55-8

Unless noted otherwise, scripture quotations are from The ESV®Bible (The Holy Bible, English Standard Version®), copyright © 2001 by Crossway. Used by permission. All rights reserved.

Scripture quotations taken from The Holy Bible, New International Version® NIV®, Copyright © 1973, 1978, 1984, 2011 by Biblica, Inc.™ Used by permission. All rights reserved worldwide.

To Asher,
praying you bow the knee to
King Jesus
at a very early age.
You bring me great joy

TABLE OF CONTENTS

PART I
THEOLOGICAL FOUNDATIONS FOR NEW COVENANT ETHICS

In Part I, we will explore several facets of new covenant ethics.

Chapter 1:

Introduction

What is Christian Ethics?

Christian ethics is about "life under the lordship of Christ." In Luke 6:46, Jesus said, "Why do you call me 'Lord, Lord,' and not do what I tell you?" Ethics is about kingdom living. The gospel announces the in-breaking of the kingdom. Therefore the evangel brings with it an ethic because we must submit to the king to enter the kingdom. To talk about ethics is not so much about asking "what to do?" but "whose are we?" As Lee Camp writes, "Claiming Jesus as Lord results in a particular manner of life, for which Jesus is the authority. In other words, the claim 'Jesus is Lord' was not for them [the early Christians] merely a 'matter of doctrine,' empty of moral meaning. Confessing 'Jesus is Lord' means taking Jesus seriously as Lord, as the authority for the believer."[1]

My ethics professor at The Southern Baptist Theological Seminary, Dr. Ken Magnuson, defines Christian ethics as "the discipline that examines human character, conduct, and the purpose for human life, in conformity to and grounded in the character, will, and purposes of God as revealed in Scripture, embodied in Jesus Christ, and established in the created order, and which is made possible by the power of the Holy Spirit." This is a good and thorough definition, but we could also describe Christian ethics simply as the discipline that shows Christians how to live *Chris-*

---

[1] Lee Camp, *Mere Discipleship* (Grand Rapids: Brazos, 2003), 125.

tianly. Obeying the teachings of Jesus and living as he lived is simply what the term *Christian* means. *Disciple* simply means *learner.* A disciple is one who follows a master or teacher to learn how they should live and conduct their life.[2]

My favorite ethics definition comes from Reformed Theologian John Frame. He writes, "Ethics is theology, viewed as a means of determining which persons, acts, and attitudes receive God's blessing and which do not."[3] This definition is helpful because it maintains the biblical truth that theology and ethics go hand in hand. In this regard, I appreciate David Wells' definition of theology: "the work of bringing the truth of God's Word into lively intersection with the life of the church, as it exists in its own culture, with the intention of seeing Christian understanding, character, and behavior made more authentic. It is also the work of readying the church to speak effectively to its world, to speak in ways that are germane to that world."[4] One can see how this could also fit as a definition for Christian ethics. All true theology is practical, and all practical living must be grounded in theology.

Why Study Christian Ethics?

Why should a Christian study ethics? The **first** reason, as with the reason for all we do, is to glorify God. First Corinthians 10:31 famously says, "So, whether you eat or drink, or whatever you do, do all to the glory of God." "Do it all for the glory of God" could also be a helpful definition for Christian ethics. We should work at making every aspect of

---

[2] Camp, *Mere Discipleship,* 105.

[3] John Frame, *The Doctrine of the Christian Life* (Phillipsburg, NJ: P&R, 2008), 10.

[4] David Wells, *Losing Our Virtue* (Grand Rapids: Eerdmans, 1998), 2.

our lives honoring to God. Obviously, this includes how we live. We study ethics in order to better know how to glorify God in our daily lives.

Second, we should study Christian ethics to be biblical. The Bible is *full* of moral teaching.[5] Probably the most famous passage about the *purpose* of Scripture is 2 Timothy 3:16-17. Those verses read, "All Scripture is breathed out by God and profitable for teaching, for reproof, for correction, and for training in righteousness, that the man of God may be competent, equipped for every good work." Notice the ethical wording: correcting, training, righteousness, equipped, and good work. Also notice the purpose given: *so that* the servant of God may be thoroughly equipped for good works. John Frame is therefore right to say that *everything* in the Bible is ethical.[6] Even when the Bible is teaching things Christians ought to believe, it is ethical: we *ought* to believe the things God has revealed.[7] Or as Frame puts it, "All the content of Scripture ought to be believed and acted upon."[8]

This is one of the reasons that the Christian faith is not called a system, a set of beliefs, a philosophy, or a worldview. The book of Acts often describes the Christian faith as "the Way" (9:2, 18:25-26, 19:9, 23, 24:14, 22), meaning a certain way of life. As Camp puts it, "To understand

---

[5] Michael Hill, *The How and Why of Love* (Australia: Matthias Media, 2002), 15.

[6] Frame, *The Doctrine of the Christian Life*, 4.

[7] Epistemology should be regarded as a branch of ethics. See John Frame, *The Doctrine of the Knowledge of God* (Phillipsburg, NJ: P&R, 1987), 63.

[8] Frame, *The Doctrine of the Christian Life*, 5.

that Jesus is the Messiah entails a particular lifestyle or a particular *way*, namely the way of the Messiah."[9]

A **third** reason is to help us live distinctly Christian lives in a fallen world. We are the people of the living God. We should be *different*. The church is God's alternate society; God's pilgrim people. We are resident aliens. We have kingdom values and seek to make something of God's kingdom visible in our lives, actions, and words. Through our corporate life, we erect signs of God's reign.[10] One pastor writes, "Living under the reign of God, as modeled by Jesus, is as contrary to the ordinary way of doing life as anything could be. It's far more radical and countercultural than most people realize, so much so that it would be impossible for someone to live this way by their own power."[11] We live counterculturally because we have the empowering presence of God. The prophets spoke of a day when God would pour out his Spirit on all people (Joel 2, Isa. 32:15, 44:3). Yahweh would do this when he restored his people. In the last days, God would pour out his Spirit and raise his people from the dead (Ezek. 36-37). God began to fulfill these promises in the resurrection of Jesus and the pouring out of the Spirit at Pentecost. The church is the end-time people of God. We are those on whom the culmination of the ages has come (1 Cor. 10:11). The church embodies the new order, the new world-on-the-way.[12] As Leslie Newbig-

---

[9] Camp, *Mere Discipleship*, 36.

[10] Michael W. Goheen and Craig G. Bartholomew, *Living at the Crossroads* (Grand Rapids: Baker Academic, 2008), 60.

[11] Greg Boyd, *The Myth of a Christian Religion* (Grand Rapids: Zondervan, 2009), 17. The reader should know that I do not endorse Boyd's view of the relationship between human freedom and God's sovereignty.

[12] Camp, *Mere Discipleship*, 106, 149.

in put it, the church is to be the sign, the agent, and the first fruits of the kingdom.[13]

How could we, as the eschatological people of the one true Lord, live just like the rest of the world? Ron Sider puts it well, "The church is a new, visible social order. It is a radical new community visibly living a challenge to the sexual insanity, the racial and social prejudice, and the economic injustice that pervade the rest of society. The church, as Rodney Clapp says so well in *A Peculiar People,* is a new way of living together in community."[14]

A **fourth** reason the study of ethics is important is because of the nature of saving faith. We Westerners tend to have a distorted view of faith. Many think it has to do with mere intellectual assent, but this is more Greek than biblical. True faith is never static, but is, as Luther put it, "a busy little thing." We tend to reduce the nature of faith and grace. Grace is not *merely* pardon, but also power.[15] Let us not cheapen either. As Bonhoeffer famously put it, "The only man who has the right to say that he is justified by grace alone is the man who has left all to follow Christ. Such a man knows that the call to discipleship is a gift of grace, and that the call is inseparable from the grace. But those who try to use this grace as a dispensation from following Christ are simply deceiving themselves.... The word of cheap grace has been the ruin of more Christians than any command-

---

[13] Leslie Newbigin, *The Gospel in a Pluralist Society* (Grand Rapids: Eerdmans, 1989), 87.

[14] Ronald J. Sider, *The Scandal of the Evangelical Conscience* (Grand Rapids: Baker, 2005), 103.

[15] See John Reisinger, *Grace* (Frederick, MD: New Covenant Media, 2008).

ment of works."[16] Ron Sider echoes Bonhoeffer: "Cheap grace results when we reduce the gospel to forgiveness of sins; limit salvation to personal fire insurance against hell; misunderstand persons as primarily souls; at best, grasp only half of what the Bible says about sin; embrace the individualism, materialism, and relativism of our current culture; lack a biblical understanding and practice of the church; and fail to teach a biblical worldview."[17]

Part of the problem is an overemphasis on the doctrine of justification *to the neglect* of the Bible's teaching on transformation and renewal.[18] For example, Reformed theologian Michael Horton says, "As heretical as it sounds today, it is probably worth telling Americans that you don't need Jesus

---

[16] Dietrich Bonhoeffer, *The Cost of Discipleship* (New York: Simon & Schuster, 1995), 51, 55.

[17] Ronald Sider, *The Scandal of the Evangelical Conscience,* 56; New Testament scholar Michael Gorman similarly writes, "Today, once again, many Christians and churches face the temptations of cultural captivity, 'spirituality' without discipleship or ethics, and knee-jerk nationalism. These are all forms of cheap grace, or cheap justification — a relationship with God in which God is believed to be a kind of cosmic agent of 'salvation' (happiness, blessing, security, prosperity, etc.) who requires little or nothing of the allegedly 'saved' or 'blessed.' Cheap justification is justification without transformation, without conversion, without justice. Once again, someone needs to speak, not merely of grace, but of *costly* grace; not merely justification by faith, but of *costly* justification by faith," in *Reading Paul* (Eugene, OR: Cascade, 2008), 112.

[18] I avoid the word "sanctification" because the Bible does not always use the word the way systematic theology typically uses it. Most of the time, the Bible refers to positional sanctification while systematic theology usually means a process. See David Peterson, *Possessed by God* (Downers Grove, IL: IVP, 1995).

to have better families, finances, health, or even morality."[19] In this book, Horton is calling the American evangelical church back to the message of justification—and I agree she needs a fresh dose—but is it really true that we don't need Jesus (or his Spirit) to have better morality? I don't think so. Personally, my stewardship, parenting, and marriage would look much different without Jesus. I love the doctrine of justification, but it needs to be pointed out that this is one of many metaphors the apostle uses to describe our salvation. Justification language is only unpacked in 2 out of 27 letters of the New Testament. An overemphasis on forgiveness of sins *to the neglect* of transformation can unintentionally lead to easy-believism. The mere "transaction" view of salvation has been detrimental to the people of God.[20] As Lee Camp puts it, "'Salvation,' instead of being construed as the gift of a transformed, abundant life in the now-present kingdom of God, begins to be equated with an otherworldly reward. More crassly put, 'salvation' is increasingly viewed as a fire-insurance policy—rather than the gift of new life in the here and now that stands confident even in the face of

---

[19] Michael Horton, *Christless Christianity* (Grand Rapids: Baker, 2008), 94. Later on, he writes, "People may get a lot better financial, marital, and child-rearing advice from wise uncles and aunts or even non-Christian neighbors than from their pastor. Rather, ministers are trained to be wise in the Scriptures, which center on the drama of redemption," 146-47. One can only hope that pastors and minsters will not adopt such a pastoral philosophy that would lead to a so-called "drama of redemption" that left out the vast implications of this drama on the details of life.

[20] See Darrell L. Bock, *Recovering the Real Lost Gospel* (Nashville: B&H Academic, 2010).

death."[21] The gospel is more comprehensive than that. On the cross, Christ frees us from both the *penalty* of sin and the *power* of sin.[22]

A **fifth** reason to study ethics is to develop a moral imagination. The need for a biblically informed moral imagination is great, since there are so many "gray areas" in life. Christians must learn to conduct themselves in a Christ-exalting way even in areas where there is no "word from above." Many—if not most—of the decisions we make every day lack a commandment to guide us. For these situations, we must develop the mind of Christ. New Covenant ethics is not exhaustive, like the old covenant law was. There was very little "gray area" there. There is more freedom in the new covenant. In Romans 12:1-2, Paul writes, "I appeal to you therefore, brothers, by the mercies of God, to present your bodies as a living sacrifice, holy and acceptable to God, which is your spiritual worship. Do not be conformed to this world, but be transformed by the renewal of your mind, that by testing you may discern what is the will of God, what is good and acceptable and perfect." By test-

---

[21] Camp, *Mere Discipleship,* 22. Greg Boyd similarly writes, "He's [God] not primarily about getting people to pray a magical 'sinner's prayer' or to confess certain magical truths as a means of escaping hell. He's not about gathering together a group who happen to believe all the right things. Rather, he's about gathering together a group of people who embody the kingdom—who individually and corporately manifest the reality of the reign of God on the earth," in *The Myth of a Christian Nation* (Grand Rapids: Zondervan, 2005), 30.

[22] Michael Gorman writes, "We need both forgiveness and liberation. For Paul, Christ's death accomplishes both: it is God's way of both forgiving our sins (plural) and liberating us from the power of sin (singular) by defeating its death-dealing power (Rom. 3:21-26; 8:1-4)" in *Reading Paul,* 87.

ing, *you* discern the will of God. Similarly, in Philippians 1:9-10, Paul writes, "And it is my prayer that your love may abound more and more, with knowledge and all discernment, so that you may approve what is excellent." Part of renewing the mind is developing a moral imagination. We renew our minds so we can test and approve God's will. Or consider Galatians 5:16, where Paul says, "But I say, walk by the Spirit, and you will not gratify the desires of the flesh." New Testament scholar Gordon Fee calls this "Paul's basic ethical imperative."[23]

A **sixth** and final reason to study ethics is mission. In Matthew 5:16, Jesus said, "In the same way, let your light shine before others, so that they may see your good works and give glory to your Father who is in heaven." Peter exhorts us to "Live such good lives among the pagans that, though they accuse you of doing wrong, they may see your good deeds and glorify God on the day he visits us" (1 Pet. 2:12 NIV). Graham Tomlin is worth quoting at length:

> The Christian who learns generosity, kindness or humility as a way of life begins to be noticed. Her friends and neighbors quietly begin to wonder why she seems different, striking, at peace. Some are offended and angered by what they assume is some kind of spiritual superiority; some are drawn to ask the question of why she is like this. The result is the glory of God and the salvation of people. If such virtue is absent, the non-Christian wonders what all the fuss is about. If Christians don't live in any discernibly different way from all the others, then why should he believe what they say? But if they do live differently, then it challenges, provokes, and intrigues. Christian virtue is, at the end of the day, a missionary imperative.

---

[23] Gordon Fee, *God's Empowering Presence* (Peabody, MA: Hendrickson, 1994), 429.

This is a crucial point to grasp. The true motivation for growth in spiritual fitness is not that we feel better. It is that God is glorified in us. As Christian people and communities learn a new way of life, become capable of remaining patient, faithful, and generous despite everything life throws at them, that begins to provoke questions, which of course leads to fruitful evangelism. It is only when growth in holiness—spiritual fitness—is placed in this context as the key to mission, that it finds its proper place and stops leading us back into an anxious search for salvation through our own efforts, leading to the spiritual equivalent of constantly stepping onto the scales to check whether we really are losing weight or not. The work of Christ frees us from that. It makes us relaxed, joyful, at peace. It also encourages us to pursue spiritual fitness not for our own sake but so that others see it and are drawn to the Christ who inspires it.[24]

Ethics is also a good way to discuss the gospel with unbelievers. Most people do not care to talk about the Bible today or the rational proofs for God's existence, but many people have opinions about the hot-button ethical issues of the day. Consider marriage, homosexuality, war, abortion, euthanasia, genetic research, suicide, and so on. Tied to this is apologetics. As John Frame puts it, "The main currents of twentieth- and twenty-first-century thought have become

---

[24] Graham Tomlin, *Spiritual Fitness* (New York: Continuum, 2006), 104; Lee Camp similarly writes, "In other words, throughout the biblical narrative God calls his people to embody an alternative vision of community life: the people of God live a community ethic that stands at odds with the unbelieving peoples that surround them. Through being a 'peculiar people,' the people of God can bear witness to the will of God, as well as bring about transformative change for the cities in which they dwell. Only by being what God has called his people to be can his people really bring about good for the cities in which they dwell," in *Mere Discipleship*, 83.

bankrupt, confessedly unable to provide any basis for distinguishing right from wrong. I believe that many people today are hungering for answers and are even willing to look at religious positions to find them."[25] We need to be ready to talk with such people. More reasons could be listed for why ethics is worth studying, but if you are reading this book you probably don't need any more!

---

[25] Frame, *The Doctrine of the Christian Life*, 5.

Chapter 2:

Worldview

One's worldview will determine one's ethics. What, then, is a worldview? The term is a translation of the German word *weltanschauung*, meaning a way of looking at the world (*welt* = world; *schauen* = to look).[26] It is the comprehensive grid through which we perceive reality.[27] In his classic book, *The Universe Next Door*, James Sire defines a worldview as "a commitment, a fundamental orientation of the heart, that can be expressed as a story or in a set of presuppositions (assumptions which may be true, partially true, or entirely false) which we hold (consciously or subconsciously, consistently or inconsistently) about the basic constitution of reality, as that provides the foundation on which we live and move and have our being."[28] Albert Wolters defines a worldview as "the comprehensive framework of one's basic beliefs about things."[29] My pre-

---

[26] Nancy Pearcey, *Total Truth* (Wheaton, IL: Crossway, 2005), 23. Pearcey's book is probably the current "go to" book on worldview in my opinion.

[27] N.T. Wright, *The New Testament and the People of God* (Minneapolis: Fortress, 1992), 38.

[28] James W. Sire, *The Universe Next Door* (Downers Grove, IL: IVP Academic, 2004), 17.

[29] Albert M. Wolters, *Creation Regained* (Grand Rapids: Eerdmans, 2005), 2. Greg Bahnsen define a worldview as "a network of presuppositions which are not tested by natural science and in terms of which all experience is related and interpreted," *Pushing the Antithesis* (Powder Springs, GA: American Vision, 2007), 42. In an earlier book, Bahnsen defined a worldview as "a network of related presupposi-

ferred definition comes from Michael Goheen and Craig Bartholomew. They write:

> Worldview is an articulation of the basic beliefs embedded in a shared grand story that are rooted in a faith commitment and that give shape and direction to the whole of our individual and corporate lives.[30]

Every living person has a worldview. It is simply part of being a human being.[31] All people have a set of convictions about how reality functions and how they should live in that reality.[32] Our worldview informs how we approach religion, ethics, education, politics, environmental concerns, health care, family, dress, and entertainment. Worldviews provide a model *of the world* which guides its adherents *in the world*.[33]

A helpful way to discern what our worldview is by asking five fundamental questions:[34]

---

tions in terms of which every aspect of man's knowledge and awareness is interpreted," *Always Ready* (Nacogdoches, TX: Covenant Media Press, 2006), 119-20.

[30] Michael W. Goheen and Craig G. Bartholomew, *Living at the Crossroads* (Grand Rapids: Baker Academic, 2008), 23.

[31] Wolters, *Creation Regained,* 4.

[32] Pearcey, *Total Truth,* 23.

[33] Brian J. Walsh and Richard Middleton, *The Transforming Vision* (Downers Grove, IL: IVP, 1984), 32.

[34] I am indebted to N.T. Wright, *Jesus and the Victory of God* (Minneapolis: Fortress, 1996), 443-74, for these questions. As far as I can tell, these originate in Middleton and Walsh, *The Transforming Vision,* 35, but they stopped with question four. Wright originally only had four, (*The New Testament and the People of God* [Minneapolis: Fortress, 1992], 132-33) but added the fifth in *Jesus and the Victory of God* (Minneapolis: Fortress, 1996), 138. So also Craig G. Bartholomew and Mi-

1. Who are We?
2. Where are We?
3. What's Wrong?
4. What's the Solution?
5. What Time is it?

All people have answers to these questions, but the Christian has definite, specific, and consistent answers to each of these:[35]

1. Who are We?—Image Bearers: Humans are the apex (*not* ex-ape) of creation. We are image bearers of the one true creator with responsibilities that accompany that status.

2. Where are We?—God's Good, but Fallen World: We are in a good and beautiful, though badly broken, world, the creation of the God in whose image we are made.

3. What's Wrong?—The Fall: Humanity has rebelled against its maker. This rebellion reflects a cosmic dislocation between the creator and the creation.

4. What's the Solution?—Jesus: The creator has acted, is acting, and will act within his creation through his Son to deal with the weight of evil set up by human rebellion, and to bring his world to the end for which he made it, namely that it should resonate fully with his presence and glory.

5. What Time is it?—The Last Days: We live in the overlap of the ages. The kingdom has come in Jesus, but

[35] Wright, *The New Testament and the People of God,* 132-33.

will not be fully consummated until he returns to renew the world.

An unbeliever will have various answers to these questions. In my experience, their answers will usually be inconsistent. This presents a wonderful opportunity to ask pene-
trating questions to show the bankruptcy of any and all
non-Christian worldviews and proceed with the gospel's
solution.

Apologetics

It is important to see that the Christian faith uniquely has
a basis for *any* discussion of ethics.[36] This fact presents us
with a wonderful apologetic opportunity. Conceptually,
cultural relativism reigns. As Allan Bloom famously put it
in 1987, "There is one thing a professor can be absolutely
certain of: almost every student entering the university believes, or says he believes, that truth is relative."[37] Theologian David Wells writes, "People can believe what they want
and, within the law, do what they want, but it becomes in-
tolerable if they imagine that what they believe includes
standards of belief and morality that are applicable to others. Today, that is the unforgivable sin. It is the blasphemy
against the (secular) spirit."[38]

Consider these words from the *Humanist Manifesto*
(1973): "We affirm that moral values derive their source
from human experience. Ethics is autonomous and situa-

---

[36] See how Douglas Wilson beats this dead horse against former atheist
   Christopher Hitchens in *Is Christianity Good for the World* (Moscow,
   ID: Canon Press, 2008), 40, 41, 47, 64-65.

[37] Allan Bloom, *The Closing of the American Mind* (New York: Simon &
   Schuster, 1987), 25.

[38] Wells, *Losing Our Virtue,* 51.

tional needing no theological or ideological sanction. Ethics stems from human need and interest." Or consider these words from French researcher Emile Durkheim: "It can no longer be maintained nowadays that there is one, single morality which is valid for all men at all times in all places.... The purpose of morality practiced by a people is to enable it to live; hence morality changes with societies. There is not just one morality, but several, and as many as there are social types. And as our societies change, so will our morality." A teen publication called "The Quest for Excellence" says, "Early on in life, you will be exposed to different value systems from your family, church or synagogue, and friends.... It is up to you to decide upon your own value system to build your own ethical code.... You will have to learn what is right for yourself through experience.... Only you can decide what is right and comfortable for you."[39] Yale University law professor, Arthur Allen Leff writes, "I will put the current situation as sharply as possible: there is today no way of 'proving' that napalming babies is bad except by asserting it (in a louder and louder voice), or by defining it as so, early in one's game, and then later slipping it through, in a whisper, as a conclusion. Now this is a fact of modern intellectual life so well and painfully known as to be one of the few which is simultaneously horrifying and banal."[40]

All moral decisions end up being either communally informed or simply a matter of personal choice. Should I help

---

[39] The quotations from this paragraph are taken from Bahnsen, *Pushing the Antithesis*, 168-69, 171.

[40] Arthur Allen Leff, "Economic Analysis of Law: Some Realism About Nominalism," *Virginia Law Review* (1974), 454-455, quoted in Bahnsen, *Pushing the Antithesis*, 171-72.

the old lady across the street or shove her into traffic? Personal choice. Should I save an abandoned litter of kittens or throw them into a wood-burning stove? Personal choice. You get the picture. It has become extremely unpopular to declare absolute truths. Feeling has replaced belief. It is okay to feel, but not okay to believe.[41] Yet at the same time, people are making moral judgments *all* the time. Eavesdrop in a crowded public place for five minutes, and you will hear a moral judgment. Even though ethical relativism is the reigning view of ethics today, people cannot live this way. As Schaeffer used to put it, they bump into reality at every point. On this point, they are dreadfully inconsistent.

Part of our goal is to make people become conscious of their beliefs (epistemologically self-conscious) and their inconsistency. We seek to deconstruct their worldview so they can better hear the claims of Christ. As we saw in the introduction, epistemology is a branch of ethics.[42] We *ought* to believe what is true. The moral relativist is making a moral claim. They are saying we *ought* to believe that there are no moral absolutes, schizophrenically having a morality about no morality. This is illustrated by the professor who denies moral absolutes but is not okay with his students cheating on his exams.[43]

---

[41] Wells, *Losing Our Virtue*, 107.

[42] Frame, *The Doctrine of the Knowledge of God*, 63; Greg L. Bahnsen, *Van Til's Apologetic* (Phillipsburg, NJ: P&R, 1998), 263.

[43] Bahnsen, *Pushing the Antithesis*, 172.

Chapter 3:

Three Schools of Christian Ethics

Historically, there have been three schools of ethics: deontological, teleological, and virtue ethics. Deontological ethics considers an act right or wrong because it should be done. This could be because it keeps a promise, it is just, or because God commands it.[44] As Michael Hill writes, "Deontological theories argue that there are certain features of actions like murder or adultery that make them right or wrong, and therefore binds people to do them (or not). All deontological theories agree that people ought to do the right thing simply because it is right, and not because of any consequences or outcomes that might follow."[45] This is a "duty-based" ethic. The main advocate for this approach was Immanuel Kant (1724-1804).

Teleological theories include consequentialism and utilitarianism. What is morally good or bad is determined by the end it brings about. Michael Hill writes, "A teleological ethic gives accounts of why actions are morally right or wrong in terms of the goals envisaged."[46] This is a "results-based" ethic. Popular advocates include Jeremy Bentham, J.S. Mill, and G.E. Moore.

Virtue ethics is more concerned with the actor's *being* than with their actions. This view maintains that right ac-

---

[44] John S. Feinberg and Paul D. Feinberg, *Ethics for a Brave New World 2nd ed.* (Wheaton, IL: Crossway, 2010), 35.

[45] Hill, *The How and Why of Love*, 25.

[46] Ibid., 26.

tions come from right sorts of people. The four cardinal virtues are wisdom, moderation, courage, and justice. The theological virtues are faith, hope, and love. This is a "character-based" ethic. Virtue ethics can be traced back to Aristotle.

Should the Christian adopt one of these three schools? Many in the past have. The deontological approach is attractive to some. For them, God has said it, and we need to do it. This position should only be attractive at first glance, however. Jesus had all sorts of harsh words for those who kept the externals of the law but whose hearts were stony. Still, there is obviously truth in this theory because we *ought* to do what God has commanded.

We also see the truthfulness of the teleological approach. One simply has to turn to a proverb to see that moral outcomes count. A good act is one that brings glory to God, which is happily also our good. Virtue ethics is also true from a Christian perspective. Good fruit comes from good trees. A good act comes from a good person.[47]

Therefore, we see that the Christian view encompasses all three of these. There is no need to try to squeeze Christian ethics into one of the three schools. Nor is there a need to pit these against each other.[48] God is concerned with the act, the outcome, and the actor. As Graham Cole puts it, "The holy God is interested in the moral agent, the moral action, and the moral aftermath."[49]

---

[47] Frame, *The Doctrine of the Christian Life,* 49-53.

[48] Ibid., 31, 33-34, 240.

[49] Graham Cole, *He Who Gives Life* (Wheaton, IL: Crossway, 2007), 246. John Frame writes, "Only God can guarantee the coherence of the three perspectives. The biblical God declares the moral law (the de-

ontological perspective), and he creates human beings to find their happiness (the teleological perspective) in obeying that law. He also makes us so that at our best we will find God's law to be our chief delight (the existential perspective [what I am labeling virtue]). So God made all three perspectives, and he made them to cohere," *The Doctrine of the Christian Life*, 123. As a New Covenant theologian, of course, I take issue with Frame's view of moral law.

Chapter 4:

Sources of Authority

As we consider the topic of Christian ethics, the question of authority is a very important one. What are the sources of moral authority for the Christian?

Reason

Under the rubric of reason, we include those aspects of creation that have a bearing on ethics (general revelation, natural law, being image bearers, and conscience). Reason is useful as a source of moral decision-making in that it aids us in understanding the reasonableness of God's written revelation.[50] It enables us to *think* God's thoughts after him, as Van Til would often say. Having the ability to reason is *part* of what it means to be made in the image of God. As those made in the image of God, we are morally responsible before him.[51]

God's moral will, or what Luther called "the natural law," is written on the heart of all people by nature.[52] God has built morality into the world and into human nature.[53] In Romans 1, Paul writes, "For the wrath of God is revealed from heaven against all ungodliness and unrighteousness of men, who by their unrighteousness suppress the truth. For

---

[50] Feinberg and Feinberg, *Ethics for a Brave New World*, 37.

[51] David Cook, *The Moral Maze* (London: SPCK, 1983), 51.

[52] Luther, "How Christians Should Regard Moses," in *Martin Luther's Basic Theological Writings*, ed. Timothy F. Lull, (Minneapolis: Fortress Press, 1989), 138.

[53] Cook, *The Moral Maze,* 51.

what can be known about God is plain to them, because God has shown it to them" (vv. 18-19).... Though they know God's decree that those who practice such things deserve to die, they not only do them but give approval to those who practice them" (v. 32). In Romans 2:26, Paul uses this same word *"dikaiōma"*: "So, if a man who is uncircumcised keeps the precepts (*dikaiōmata*) of the law, will not his uncircumcision be regarded as circumcision?" In Romans 2:14-15, Paul writes, "For when Gentiles, who do not have the law, by nature do what the law requires, they are a law to themselves, even though they do not have the law. They show that the work of the law is written on their hearts, while their conscience also bears witness, and their conflicting thoughts accuse or even excuse them." God's decree is known to all. All have the work of the law written on their hearts. Natural law is grounded in creation and expresses God's character.

It is important to note that natural law is insufficient to save. Unbelievers are hostile to it and seek to suppress it (Rom. 1). Some natural law ethicists (mostly Thomists) are very optimistic about building a universal ethic based on natural law, but I see it as insufficient. It is one small piece of the puzzle. It often confirms the teaching of Scripture, but without Scripture, it is inadequate. I am more pessimistic, but I hope it is a biblically informed pessimism. Human nature is too fallen.

Likewise, conscience is a means the Spirit uses to help us act in a manner that pleases God, but for unbelievers, the conscience is no guide at all, as it can become evil, weak, and seared (1 Cor. 8:7, 10, 12, Heb. 10:22, 1 Tim. 4:2). Reason, therefore, is an important source of moral authority, but by itself, it is woefully inadequate.

Tradition

Tradition is also very important. We stand on the shoulders of many who have gone before and should take the church's stance on moral issues seriously as we develop our own. The Holy Spirit has a history and has been at work in the church for over 2,000 years. This obviously does not mean that we simply swallow everything the church has taught. One thinks of slavery. There were many Christians in the South who advocated slavery. As with all tradition, we examine it in light of Scripture. God's Word is the norming norm.

Experience

Since not all moral issues are black and white in Scripture, one has to walk in wisdom in many cases. We must "walk by the Spirit" (Gal. 5:16). We must continually renew the mind to discern the will of God in such cases (Rom. 12:1). As with tradition, one's experience must ultimately be examined in light of Scripture. Experience is often misleading. For example, I recall a woman who was sure she was supposed to leave her husband. She thought, "Surely God wouldn't want me in *this* difficult relationship. I feel at peace about leaving." This woman was elevating her experience above the Word of God (her reasons for wanting a divorce were not warranted by Scripture).

Scripture

While we value reason, tradition, and experience, the Holy Scriptures are the "bottom line" of the moral decision-making process.[54] We learn about God's character and ways in the Old Testament and are bound to the many imperatives of the New Testament.

---

[54] John Jefferson Davis, *Evangelical Ethics* (Phillipsburg, NJ: P&R, 2004), 15.

It is vital to realize where we are in the story in order to play our role well. We need to know what stage it is in the drama in order to participate faithfully. This is particularly important in discerning the Christian's relation to the Old Testament. Michael Hill writes, "Only a proper understanding of the whole Bible will answer the question about the validity and application of the moral elements of the law."[55] There are various ways to talk about the story of Scripture. A popular and helpful way summarizes the story under four headings:

Creation—Fall—Redemption—New Creation

In this schema, we are obviously currently in the "redemption" era. Another way to trace the story line of Scripture is by walking through the biblical covenants starting with God's creation purpose:

Creation—Noah—Abraham—Moses—David—New Covenant

Within this schema, we are obviously under the new covenant. Or consider the story of Scripture—which is the true story of the world—as five acts:[56]

Act 1: Creation

Act 2: The Fall

Act 3: God with Israel

---

[55] Michael Hill, *The How and Why of Love,* 45.

[56] Here I am indebted to Alan Kreider and Eleanor Kreider, *Worship and Mission after Christendom* (Scottsdale, PA: Herald Press, 2011), 63. I think the 5-act model was original with N.T. Wright. See his *The New Testament and the People of God,* 141-43; also see Bartholomew and Goheen, *The Drama of Scripture,* 27, who slightly modified Wright's scheme.

Act 4: Jesus' life, teaching, miracles, death, and resurrection

Act 5: Pentecost and Beyond

Scene 1—the New Testament church

Scene 2—the church throughout history (including our denomination, congregations, and missional expansion)

Scene 3—

Scene 4—future history

New Creation

Notice that scene 3 is left blank. This is because this is our time. We live in light of the first five acts and in anticipation of the final phase of new creation. We live between the two comings of Christ. As Kreider and Kreider put it, "We improvise in light of the past that we remember and the future that we hope for."[57] Our calling is to now reflect on, draw out, and implement the significance of the first five acts.[58] This means the new covenant people of God must be very familiar with God's past work. He has revealed himself in deeds and words that explain those deeds which are recorded for us in Holy Scripture. We must be people of the book. We must understand how God has worked to know how we should "work."

For the question of ethics, it is vitally important for us to know where we are in the story. We are under the new covenant, not the old covenant. With the coming of Christ, the old covenant has become obsolete (Heb. 8). This means that we are no longer bound by the Mosaic law. It was part of a

---

[57] Kreider and Kreider, *Worship and Mission,* 64.

[58] Wright, *The New Testament and the People of God,* 143.

suzerainty-vassal treaty that God made with a particular West Semitic nation living along the southeastern coast of the Mediterranean Sea.[59] We are not bound to the law *covenantally*, and we are unable to obey most of it *culturally*. Let me illustrate this latter point by a few random examples: People love to point to Leviticus 20:13 to condemn homosexuality as detestable, but what about verse 9 of the same chapter that says that children who curse their parents should be put to death? Verse 25 of the same chapter says that we must make a distinction between clean and unclean animals. Do we do this? If not, why not? What makes verse 13 binding but verses 9 and 25 culturally conditioned? Or consider Leviticus 19. Advocates of Covenant Theology[60] say we are bound only to the moral aspects of the law, but in a chapter like Leviticus 19, the command to love your neighbor (19:18) is followed by the command not to wear clothing woven of two kinds of material (19:19). How do we know that verse 18 is moral but verse 19 isn't? Deuteronomy 22:8 commands God's people to build a parapet around your roof, but this only makes sense within the world of ancient Israel where there were flat roofs where people hung out. Are we to obey this command? My roof is rather steep.

Exodus 20:8 says God's people should make sure their slave takes Saturday off. What is a Christian living in 2011 to do with such a command? Exodus 20:9 commands the Israelites to work six days, but almost every Christian I know works five days, not six. Exodus 29:22 commands them to take the fat of the ram tail. I for one cannot keep this

---

[59] David Dorsey, "The Law of Moses and the Christian: A Compromise" *JETS* 34/3 (September 1991), 325. I am dependent upon Dorsey's article in the following paragraph.

[60] More on this in the next chapter.

command because I currently live in Houston and haven't seen any Palestinian fat-tailed sheep running around lately. I can't keep Exodus 22:5 and 29:40 because I don't own a vineyard. Exodus 23:11 says to let the land lie unplowed during the seventh year, but I cannot apply this or all of the other similar commandments outlining how to cultivate the Mediterranean olive tree and the uses of its fruit. Exodus 25-29 speaks of the production of the pomegranate, date palm, acacia, almond, cassi, cinnamon, galbanum, frankincense, hyssop, Near Eastern poplar, and bitter herbs. I am not sure if I can find all these at my local grocery store. Leviticus 23:5-20 commands the Israelites to begin harvesting the standing grain seven weeks after Passover, in May/June. This command requires a Levantine, Mediterranean, or at least a northern hemispheric geoclimatic setting. As David Dorsey summarizes, "The Sinaitic law code was very specifically designed by God to regulate the lives of the West Semitic inhabitants of the southern Levant. Nearly all the regulations of the corpus—over ninety-five percent—are so culturally specific, geographically limited, and so forth that they would be completely inapplicable, and in fact unfulfillable, to Christians living throughout the world today. This fact alone should suggest that the corpus is not legally binding upon Christians and that it cannot possibly represent the marching orders of the church."[61]

It should be clear, then, that we cannot obey the law *culturally*, but thankfully we are not bound to the law *covenantally* either. Hebrews 7:22 speaks of the better covenant that Jesus has brought about. Hebrews 8 teaches that the new covenant has replaced the old. The first one was insufficient

---

[61] Dorsey, "The Law of Moses and the Christian," 329.

(2 Cor. 3). It could not produce the people it should have. God found fault with the people of the first covenant, so he promised a new one (Heb. 8:7-8).

The fundamental source of authority for Christian ethics then is Scripture. But obviously it isn't that simple. Ethics becomes a *hermeneutical* endeavor. We have to interpret and apply Scripture rightly. We must locate ourselves within redemptive history and apply the Bible accordingly. The Old Testament remains authoritative as Scripture, but we are not bound to the old covenant. We are now bound to the ethics of the new covenant, which consists of those prescriptive principles drawn from the example of Jesus and his apostles (the central demand being love), which are meant to be worked out in specific situations by the guiding influence and empowerment of the Holy Spirit.[62] In case this sounds strange to you, I am coming from a New Covenant Theology perspective. It is worth taking the next chapter to orient you to this perspective since it has a direct bearing on new covenant ethics.

---

[62] I have modified the definitions of "the law of Christ" given by Douglas J. Moo in "The Law of Christ as the Fulfillment of the Law of Moses: A Modified Lutheran View," in *Five Views on Law and Gospel,* ed. Stanley N. Gundry (Grand Rapids: Zondervan, 1999), 343, 357, 361, 368-69 and Richard Longenecker in *Galatians* (Dallas: Word, 1990), 275-76.

Chapter 5:

A Short Primer on New Covenant Theology[63]

If this ethical perspective sounds strange or is new to you, it is because this is a "New Covenant Theological" position. It might be helpful to take a chapter to cover the "essentials" of what this theological system is all about. A very important passage for the theological system of New Covenant Theology is 1 Corinthians 9:20-21. That passage reads, "To the Jews I became as a Jew, in order to win Jews. To those under the law I became as one under the law (though not being myself under the law) that I might win those under the law. To those outside the law I became as one outside the law (not being outside the law of God but under the law of Christ) that I might win those outside the law." This helpful passage summarizes the New Covenant Theology (or better, Pauline) view of law. Paul is clear that he is not under the law (*nomos*—meaning law of Moses), but he is not free from God's law. We see, therefore, that God's law is no longer equivalent to the Mosaic law but is now Christ's law.

Currently there are three main systems of theology within evangelical Christianity: Covenant Theology, Dispensationalism, and New Covenant Theology. Generally speaking, Covenant Theologians emphasize continuity between the covenants to the expense of discontinuity. Since the

---

[63] If interested in probing a little deeper, see my *What is New Covenant Theology: An Introduction* (Frederick, MD: New Covenant Media, 2012).

Westminster Confession of Faith is structured around Covenant Theology, it is mostly Presbyterians who adhere to Covenant Theology, although others do as well (e.g. Reformed Baptists who hold to the London Baptist Confession of 1689).

Dispensationalism tends to emphasize discontinuity between the covenants to the expense of continuity. It is mostly Bible churches that adhere to Dispensationalism, but it is certainly not limited to them. Dispensationalism is by far the most popular of the three, due in large part to the popular marketing with fictional books and movies, as well as the hugely influential Scofield Reference Bible.

The third system of theology is New Covenant Theology, sometimes called "Progressive Covenantalism." It emphasizes both continuity and discontinuity. It is held to by those in the "believer's church" tradition. New Covenant Theology is a relatively new label, but it is not a new method of interpretation. The early church fathers and the Anabaptists were "putting the Bible together" in a similar way.

There is lots of diversity in each of these three systems, but each has theological positions that make them unique. There are seven key distinctives that make up New Covenant Theology. Taken by themselves, these points may fit into Covenant Theology and/or Dispensationalism, but taken together, they uniquely fit New Covenant Theology.

1. One Plan of God Centered in Jesus Christ

The first distinctive belief is that there is one plan of God throughout the Bible. This plan is centered on Jesus Christ. Ephesians 1:8-10 says, "With all wisdom and understanding, he made known to us the mystery of his will according to his good pleasure, which he purposed in Christ, to be put into effect when the times reach their fulfillment—to bring unity to all things in heaven and on earth under Christ" (NIV). Covenant Theology speaks of this plan in terms of the "covenant of grace." New Covenant Theology strives to let *biblical* theology inform *systematic* theology. Exegesis should be the lifeblood of theology. This being the case, New Covenant Theology does not find exegetical warrant for a "covenant of grace" that encompasses all the biblical covenants. This tends to flatten out the Bible. There is both continuity between the covenants and discontinuity. Each must be dealt with in its own context. When we do this, it becomes clear that there is a sharp contrast between the old covenant and the new. Dispensationalism, on the other hand, tends to chop up the Bible, not seeing the fulfillment that the Messiah brings in continuity with what has gone before.

2. The Old Testament Should be Interpreted in Light of the New Testament

One of the hermeneutical strategies New Covenant Theology is built upon is reading the Old Testament in light of the New Testament. We take the *progressive* nature of God's revelation with the utmost seriousness (Heb. 1:1). We learn how to interpret the Old Testament from Jesus and his apostles. It is our opinion that the conclusions of Covenant Theology and Dispensationalism are a result of beginning with the Old Testament rather than the New Testament. As John G. Reisinger is fond of pointing out, both systems ironically read elements of the Abrahamic covenant in a way contrary to that of the apostles in our humble opinion.

3. The Old Covenant was Temporary by Divine Design

The third belief is that the old covenant was *temporary* by divine design. God intended for it to be an interim covenant. The New Testament is emphatic about the fact that those in Christ are no longer under the law (1 Cor. 9:20, 2 Cor. 3, Rom. 6:14, 7:6, Gal. 3:23, 5:18, Heb. 8). Galatians is very clear about this point. The Judaizers needed new "watch batteries." They failed to realize what time it was in God's plan. The Bible depicts history as being divided up between this age and the age to come. This present evil age consists of sin, flesh, and death but when the Messiah comes, he will usher in the new age of righteousness, Spirit, and life. Paul sees the old covenant law as part of the old age (Gal. 1:4, Rom. 6:14). The Judaizers were trying to force Gentile believers to observe the old covenant law. Paul insists that its day is over. The law was given *after* the promise to Abraham and *until* the Messiah came. Galatians 3:19 says, "Why then the law? It was added because of transgressions, until the offspring should come to whom the promise had been made, and it was put in place through angels by an intermediary." Verses 24-25 say, "So then, the law was our guardian until Christ came, in order that we might be justified by faith. But now that faith has come, we are no longer under a guardian." Here Paul calls the law a guardian *(paidagōgos)*. In the first century, this referred to the household slave who was responsible for a child until they reached maturity. Paul's point is temporal. Once we are grown up, we no longer need a guardian. With the coming of Christ, we have grown up. The old covenant law was an intended parenthesis in God's plan and has now been replaced by the new covenant (Heb. 8).

4. There is No Tripartite Division of the Law

Covenant Theology divides the law up into three parts: moral, civil, and ceremonial. While we see how some commandments could be classified as moral in nature, as opposed to civil or ceremonial, New Covenant Theology denies this "tripartite" division of the law because the writers of Scripture do not make such distinctions (e.g., skim through Lev. 19 and try to classify the commandments). The law is presented as a unit throughout Scripture. Hebrews 7:11-12 says, "If perfection could have been attained through the Levitical priesthood—and indeed the law given to the people established that priesthood—why was there still need for another priest to come, one in the order of Melchizedek, not in the order of Aaron? For when the priesthood is changed, the law must be changed also" (NIV). Notice that the law and the priesthood are bound up together. It is a package deal. If the priesthood changes, then the law changes as well. This three-fold division has no biblical basis. Covenant Theology likes to emphasize that the Ten Commandments are the eternal moral law of God, but the Ten Commandments cannot be extrapolated from the covenant in which they were given. A careful reading of Exodus 19-24 bears this out. Chapter 19 is the historical introduction and chapter 24 is the covenant ceremony. Chapter 20 consists of the ten words (20:1). Chapters 21-23 consist of the rules (21:1). In chapter 24, Moses calls both the words and the rules the "Book of the Covenant" (24:3, 7). One cannot have the ten words without the rules that go with them. Chapter 20 belongs with chapters 21-23.

One also must take the Sabbath commandment into account. The other nine commandments do not pose as much of a problem, since the New Testament repeats them. The New Testament does not reinforce the Sabbath command though. Quite the contrary! After the coming of Christ, observing days is akin to returning to paganism (Gal. 4:8-10). Romans 14:5 says that regarding observing special days, each should be fully convinced in their own mind. That is a far cry from "Remember the Sabbath day and keep it holy."

Paul calls the Sabbath a shadow in Colossians 2:16-17. Again, exegesis must inform our theology.

5. We are not Under the Law of Moses, but Under the Law of Christ

If we are not under the law, does that mean we are lawless? No. We are no longer under the law of Moses, but the ethics of the new covenant. As noted above, the ethics of the new covenant can be defined as those prescriptive principles drawn from the example and teaching of Jesus and his apostles (the central demand being love), which are meant to be worked out in specific situations by the guiding influence and empowerment of the Holy Spirit.[64]

6. All in the New Covenant Community Have the Holy Spirit

The sixth distinctive belief is the nature of the new covenant community. In the new covenant, unlike the old, every member is fully forgiven and every member is permanently indwelt by the Spirit. This is another way of saying they are all *believers*. The prophets looked forward to a day when God would pour out his Spirit from on high (Ezek. 36-37, Joel 2, Isa. 32, 44). This is one of the major differences between Israel and the church. Not all within Israel had the Spirit. All within the new covenant community do.

7. The Church is the Eschatological Israel

---

[64] As noted above, I have modified the definitions of the law of Christ given by Douglas J. Moo in "The Law of Christ as the Fulfillment of the Law of Moses: A Modified Lutheran View," 343, 357, 361, 368-69 and Richard Longenecker in *Galatians*, 275-76. As we will see below, I think Paul has something more specific in mind by the phrase "law of Christ" in Galatians 6:2.

New Covenant Theology does not say that Israel=church as Covenant Theology does. Neither do we make a radical distinction between Israel and the church as Dispensationalism does. Again, Jesus is the hermeneutical key! New Covenant Theology strives to be *consistently* Christocentric. The New Testament depiction is Israel=Jesus=church. Galatians 3:16 explicitly says that the seed of Abraham is singular. Believers are considered the offspring of Abraham (i.e., Israel) by being united to Jesus—the seed of Abraham. Galatians 3:7 says, "Know then that it is those of faith who are the sons of Abraham." Galatians 3:29 says, "And if you are Christ's, then you are Abraham's offspring, heirs according to promise." Galatians 6:15-16 says, "Neither circumcision nor uncircumcision means anything; what counts is the new creation. Peace and mercy to all who follow this rule—to the Israel of God" (NIV, cf. Phil. 3:2-3, Rom. 2:28-29). All of the promises of God are yes in Christ Jesus (2 Cor. 1:20).

Chapter 6:

Indicative/Imperative

Another vital aspect of new covenant ethics is grasping the relationship between the indicative and the imperative. In grammar, we speak of different types of moods. The indicative mood represents the act or state as an objective fact. For example, "the cat is on the mat" is an indicative statement. It is a fact. The cat *is* on the mat.[65] It is a statement about what *is*.

The imperative mood expresses an intention to influence the listener's behavior. It is used with commands, requests, etc. "Put the cat on the mat" is an imperative statement. You are being told to *do something* with the cat.

This grammar language has often been applied to New Testament ethics, especially with regard to Paul's letters. The indicative is what God has done for us in Christ. It is who we are in Christ. We are forgiven, reconciled, and adopted. We are "in Christ." It is a fact. We have a new status. The imperative is what we are called to do and be as those in Christ. It is what God demands of us.

The distinction between indicative and imperative is an important one, for Christianity is not simply a moralistic religion.[66] The message of Christianity is not merely "be

---

[65] I heard the "cat and mat" phrase from Michael Horton in a lecture the details of which I unfortunately cannot recall.

[66] Victor P. Furnish writes, "No interpretation of the Pauline ethic can be judged successful which does not grapple with the problem of indic-

good people," or "do the right things." The fundamental message of Christianity is that Jesus Christ has died for sinners, has been raised from the dead and exalted to the Father's right hand, and now exercises complete authority. We are called to be "good" people and do certain things *in light* of that reality.[67] This relationship is really what sets Christianity over against all other religions. Pastor Tim Keller aptly writes, "Religion operates on the principle 'I obey — therefore I am accepted by God.' But the operating principle of the gospel is 'I am accepted by God through what Christ has done — therefore I obey.'"[68] The order makes all the difference in the world!

This is another way of saying that the imperative flows from the indicative. The indicative is the foundation of the imperative. The indicative and the imperative are "closely and necessarily associated."[69] They cannot be separated without distorting the theology of the New Testament. We will be asking "what would Jesus do?" in the second half of this book, but we only ask this after we have asked and answered the question, "what did Jesus do?" As New Testament scholar Wolfgang Schrage says, "God's eschatological act of salvation in Jesus Christ is the absolute basis, foundation, and prerequisite for all Christian conduct."[70]

---

ative and imperative in Paul's thought," *Theology and Ethics in Paul* (Nashville: Abingdon, 1968), 279.

[67] As Richard Hays writes, "Moral action is a logical entailment of God's redemptive action," *The Moral Vision of the New Testament* (New York: HarperOne, 1996), 39.

[68] Tim Keller, *The Reason for God* (NY: Dutton, 2008), 179-80.

[69] Furnish, *Theology and Ethics*, 223-24.

[70] Wolfgang Schrage, *The Ethics of the New Testament* (Philadelphia: Fortress Press, 1982), 167.

Protestants have historically guarded this biblical truth by distinguishing the doctrine of justification from the doctrine of sanctification (or transformation). Justification is forensic; it is a declaration. We are declared to be in the right through faith. Faith unites us to the Messiah so that what is true of him is true of us. Historically, the doctrine of sanctification has referred to the *process* of becoming more and more like Jesus. In this sense, transformation is a process while justification is a one-time event. Our sanctification, or moral transformation, flows from our right standing, our justification.

Martin Luther guarded this distinction by speaking of the two kinds of righteousness. He distinguished passive righteousness from active righteousness. Passive righteousness is the righteous status that we are given by God through faith (Phil. 3:8-9). We are passive in receiving this righteousness. Active righteousness is the good works we are called to do in light of our righteous standard. Our behavior must match our status; our righteous status must manifest itself in righteous behavior.[71]

Now let us look at Paul's letters to show how he commands Christians to live. First, let us consider the overall structure of Paul's letters.[72] It is Paul's practice to lay out the doctrinal foundations before turning to "ethics." Consider Galatians: Paul deals with the seriousness of the Judaizers' error, the nature of Paul's calling, his apostolic authority, the implications of the gospel, his confrontation of Peter, their reception of the Holy Spirit, the role of the law in redemptive history, the natures of the Abrahamic and Old

---

[71] R.E.O. White, *Biblical Ethics* (Atlanta: John Knox Press, 1979), 148.

[72] Schrage, *The Ethics of the New Testament*, 167.

covenants, and adoption before coming to the first major imperative in 4:12: "Become as I am." Chapters 5 and 6 follow with pointed ethical exhortation.

The book of Ephesians is similar. It can be nicely divided into two sections: chapters 1-3 and chapters 4-6. Chapters 1-3 lay out the spiritual blessings in Christ for the individual and the community. After laying out a lot of doctrine, Paul urges them "to live a life worthy of the calling" they have received (4:1). The first half is about the creation of the new humanity, and the second half is about the conduct of the new humanity. The book of Romans is similar as well. There is a lot of theology in chapters 1-11. It is only after these glorious chapters that Paul writes, "I appeal to you therefore, brothers, by the mercies of God, to present your bodies as a living sacrifice" (12:1). Chapters 12-15 are heavy on gospel application.

This sort of "gospel logic" is found throughout Paul's writings. Richard Hays writes, "Consequently, much of Paul's moral exhortation takes the form of reminding his readers to view their obligations and actions in the cosmic context of what God has done in Christ."[73] He takes both the indicative and the imperative with utmost seriousness and interweaves them beautifully. Consider Romans 6; in verse 2 Paul writes that we are those who have died to sin, but in verse 11 he turns around and commands us to "count yourselves dead to sin but alive to God in Christ Jesus." He is saying in essence, "Act like what you are."[74]

---

[73] Hays, *Moral Vision*, 39.

[74] Act like what you are *becoming* is probably more accurate since we are not yet glorified. This does justice to the progressive moral transformation that must accompany our new status.

Romans 6:6 says that our old self was crucified with Christ, and Colossians 3:9-10 says we have taken off our old self; but Ephesians 4:22-24 commands us to put off our old self and to put on the new self. Again, we should act like who we are.

Colossians 3:1-5 says, "If then you have been raised with Christ, seek the things that are above, where Christ is, seated at the right hand of God. Set your minds on things that are above, not on things that are on earth. For you have died, and your life is hidden with Christ in God. When Christ who is your life appears, then you also will appear with him in glory. Put to death therefore what is earthly in you: sexual immorality, impurity, passion, evil desire, and covetousness, which is idolatry." We have been raised with Christ and therefore should set our hearts on things above. We died with Christ and therefore should put to death whatever belongs to our earthly nature. "Become what you are."

Galatians 5:1, 25, and Ephesians 5:8 contain both the indicative and the imperative in a single verse! Verse 1 of Galatians 5 reads, "For freedom Christ has set us free; stand firm therefore, and do not submit again to a yoke of slavery." A paraphrase of what Paul is saying here could be, "Christ has set us free. Be free." Behave in line with what God has done for you in Christ. Verse 25 of Galatians 5 reads, "If we live by the Spirit, let us also walk by the Spirit." In other words, "Since we live by the Spirit, let us live by the Spirit." Ephesians 5:8 reads, "For at one time you were darkness, but now you are light in the Lord. Walk as children of light" To paraphrase again: "You are children of light. Live as children of light."

Philippians 2:12-13 is a classic verse for this relationship: "Therefore, my beloved, as you have always obeyed, so now, not only as in my presence but much more in my absence, work out your own salvation with fear and trembling, for it is God who works in you, both to will and to work for his good pleasure." We are called to work because it is God at work.

Galatians 3:27 says that we who were baptized into Christ have clothed ourselves with Christ, but Romans 13:14 commands us to clothe ourselves with Christ. So clothe yourself with Christ because you *are* clothed with Christ! Become what you are.

Chapter 7:

Virtue

Virtue is an important part of new covenant ethics. To have virtue is to be a good person. Virtue is a character trait that orients or disposes a person to act in a good way.[75] C.S. Lewis writes, "We might think that God wanted simply obedience to a set of rules: whereas He really wants people of a particular sort."[76]

To grow in virtue is to become truly human. It is to act in the way we were created to act, and it is to act in the present age how we will for all eternity. We learn the language of new creation in advance. We practice the habits of the age to come.[77] As Graham Tomlin puts it, "The purpose of the gospel, then, is not just to save a few people for heaven. It is to create a new kind of person, ready to dwell in the new heavens and the new earth that are being prepared."[78]

---

[75] David VanDrunen, *BioEthics and the Christian Life* (Wheaton, IL: Crossway, 2009), 69.

[76] C.S. Lewis, *Mere Christianity* in *The Complete C.S. Lewis* (New York: HarperOne, 2002), 73.

[77] N.T. Wright writes, "This is once more the classic structure of virtue: glimpse the goal, work out the path toward it, and develop the habits which you will need to practice if you are going to tread that path," *After You Believe* (New York: HarperOne, 2010), 170.

[78] Tomlin, *Spiritual Fitness,* 81. He continues: "This means that transformation, holiness, discipleship, sanctification, spiritual fitness, or whatever you want to call it, is not an optional extra for those who take Christianity a bit more seriously than others. It is the point of the whole exercise. God forgives and rescues sinners precisely so

Being a virtuous person is a result of *practice*. As N.T. Wright says, "Virtue, in this strict sense, is what happens when someone has made a thousand small choices, requiring effort and concentration, to do something which is good and right but which doesn't come 'naturally'—and then, on the thousand and first time, when it really matters, they find that they do what's required 'automatically,' as we say."[79] This is why the little moments are so important, and why practice must happen. Take sports for example. In basketball (or golf or tennis), anyone can hit a lucky shot on occasion, but the experts nail it with ease because they have worked so hard at it. We must work hard until it becomes natural. The little decisions you and I make every day are of infinite importance!

Cardinal Virtues

The four cardinal virtues are:

- Fortitude (or courage) is pursuing what is good in the face of danger and hardship.

- Temperance (moderation, restraint) is going the right length and no further.

---

that he can turn them into people who resemble Christ and share in his image, participating in the divine nature. His purpose is to transform us into people who resemble Christ and share in his image, participating in the divine nature. His purpose is to transform us into people who are capable of fulfilling the calling he gave us at the start: to rule over creation in his name. That involves using power not for our own ends or glory, but in God's name, so that the new heaven and new earth might be peopled with those who will not (as Adam did) take the power given to them and abuse it, but will learn to rule as God does—with gentleness and justice," ibid., 81-82.

[79] Wright, *After You Believe*, 20.

- Prudence (or wisdom) means practical common sense, taking the trouble to think out what you are doing and what is likely to come of it.[80]

- Justice is the old name for everything we should now call "fairness." It includes honesty, give and take, truthfulness, and keeping your promises, etc.[81]

Theological Virtues

The three theological virtues are faith, hope, and love. These are often listed together in Paul's letters:

- 1 Corinthians 13:13: "So now faith, hope, and love abide, these three; but the greatest of these is love." It is fascinating that faith, hope, and love remain. They last into the future. They are among the things that form bridges from the present age into the age to come. These are qualities we will possess on the new earth and that we anticipate in the present.[82]

- 1 Thessalonians 1:3: "remembering before our God and Father your work of faith and labor of love and steadfastness of hope in our Lord Jesus Christ."

- 1 Thessalonians 5:8: "But since we belong to the day, let us be sober, having put on the breastplate of faith and love, and for a helmet the hope of salvation."

- Colossians 1:4-5: "since we heard of your faith in Christ Jesus and of the love that you have for all the saints, because of the hope laid up for you in heaven. Of this you have heard before in the word of the

---

[80] Lewis, *Mere Christianity*, 70.

[81] Ibid., 72.

[82] N.T. Wright, "Faith, Virtue, Justification, and the Journey to Freedom," in *The Word that Leaps the Gap*, ed. J. Ross Wagner, C. Kavin Rowe, and A. Katherine Grieb (Grand Rapids: Eerdmans, 2008), 481.

truth, the gospel." This verse states that faith and love are due to the hope we have in heaven.

Faith

The fundamental call from God to humanity is to trust him. By faith we receive the gift of righteousness. Faith is the source of all the other virtues. All other good works and virtues flow from faith (Gal. 5:6, James 2:14-26).[83] As C.S. Lewis puts it, "To trust Him [Christ] means, of course, trying to do all that He says. There would be no sense in saying you trusted a person if you would not take his advice. Thus if you have really handed yourself over to Him, it must follow that you are trying to obey Him. But trying in a new way, a less worried way. Not doing these things in order to be saved, but because He has begun to save you already. Not hoping to get to Heaven as a reward for your actions, but inevitably wanting to act in a certain way because a first faint gleam of Heaven is already inside you."[84]

Hope

Hope is closely related to faith. Hebrews 11:1 famously states, "Now faith is the assurance of things hoped for, the conviction of things not seen." The main difference is the orientation of faith and hope. Faith is oriented to the present, and hope is oriented to the future. Hope looks to the future and the promises of God yet to be received.[85] Christian hope is distinct from unbelieving hope in that it is certain and assured. Unbelieving hope is often nothing more than mere wishful thinking.

---

[83] VanDrunen, *BioEthics and the Christian Life*, 71.

[84] Lewis, *Mere Christianity*, 121.

[85] VanDrunen, *BioEthics and the Christian Life*, 75.

Sometimes Christians are criticized for being so heaven-ly-minded that they are of no earthly good. To the contrary, there is no such thing as a person who is too heavenly-minded. As Lewis writes, "If you read history, you find that the Christians who did most for the present world were just those who thought most of the next.... It is since Christians have largely ceased to think of the other world that they have become so ineffective in this. Aim at Heaven and you will get earth 'thrown in': aim at earth and you will get nei-ther."[86] The American church could use a stouter dose of heavenly-mindedness.

Love

Love is central to the Christian life. It is the first fruit of the Spirit mentioned (Gal. 5:22, cf. Rom. 12:9). As David VanDrunen writes, "Love is the preeminent Christian vir-tue, not because it can exist independently of faith and hope, but because faith and hope serve as the necessary foundation for love, that supreme work and crowning achievement of the Holy Spirit in the Christian."[87] Colos-sians 3:14 says, "And above all these put on love, which binds everything together in perfect harmony." Love is the bond that holds all the other virtues together.[88]

Love is action in the Bible. Again, Lewis writes, "But love, in the Christian sense, does not mean an emotion. It is a state not of the feelings but of the will; that state of the will which we have naturally about ourselves, and must learn to have about other people."[89] It can be defined as the giving

---

[86] Lewis, *Mere Christianity,* 112.

[87] VanDrunen, *BioEthics and the Christian Life,* 79-80.

[88] Thomas R. Schreiner, *Galatians* (Grand Rapids: Zondervan, 2010), 349.

[89] Lewis, *Mere Christianity,* 109.

of oneself for the good of others. We will spend chapters 9-15 examining this vitally important Christian virtue.

These theological virtues keep virtue ethics from being focused on the self. As Wright puts it, "But to insist that the three primary virtues are faith, hope, and above all love is to insist that to grow in these virtues is precisely to grow in *looking away from oneself* and toward God on the one hand and one's neighbor on the other. The more you cultivate these virtues, the less you will be thinking about yourself at all."[90]

Other Virtues

What are some other New Testament virtues? One thinks first of the other fruit of the Spirit: joy, peace, forbearance, kindness, goodness, gentleness, faithfulness, and self-control. Much could be said for each of these.

Wisdom is another important Christian virtue. One should peruse the book of Proverbs to grow in wisdom. Wisdom is the ability to understand how the world works.[91] Christ is the wisdom of God (1 Cor. 1:24), so growing in wisdom is growing in the mind of Christ. We need this wisdom to make ethical decisions. Another way of speaking of wisdom is to speak of "sanctified common sense."

Modesty is an attitude or pattern of behavior which expresses restraint and avoids ostentatious display. It is to avoid excess.[92] First Timothy 2:9-10 says, "Likewise also that

---

[90] Wright, *After You Believe*, 204, 205.

[91] VanDrunen, *BioEthics and the Christian Life*, 91.

[92] D.H. Field, "Modesty," in *New Dictionary of Christian Ethics and Pastoral Theology*, ed. David J. Atkinson, David F. Field, Arthur Homes, and Oliver O'Donovan (Downers Grove, IL: IVP Academic, 1995), 599.

women should adorn themselves in respectable apparel, with modesty and self-control, not with braided hair and gold or pearls or costly attire, but with what is proper for women who profess godliness—with good works."

Humility is also very important. Isaiah 66:2 reads, "All these things my hand has made, and so all these things came to be, declares the LORD. But this is the one to whom I will look: he who is humble and contrite in spirit and trembles at my word." James 4:6 says that God opposes the proud but shows favor to the humble. Historically, humility was not a virtue but a vice. Lowliness of mind was frowned upon. It was good to be proud of yourself or your city in Greco-Roman culture. Not so for the Christian. We should be the humblest of all people. C.J. Mahaney, in his fantastic book on humility, defines it as "honestly assessing ourselves in light of God's holiness and our sinfulness."[93] Mahaney helpfully lists ways to weaken pride and cultivate humility:

Always:

1. Reflect on the wonder of the cross of Christ.

As each day begins:

1. Begin your day by acknowledging your dependence upon God and your need for God.

2. Begin your day expressing gratefulness to God.

3. Practice the spiritual disciplines—prayer, study of God's Word, worship. Do this consistently each day and at the day's outset, if possible.

4. Seize your commute time to memorize and meditate on Scripture.

---

[93] C.J. Mahaney, *Humility* (Colorado Springs: Multnomah, 2005), 22.

5. Cast your cares upon him, for he cares for you.

As each day ends:

1. At the end of the day, transfer the glory to God.
2. Before going to sleep, receive this gift of sleep from God and acknowledge his purpose for sleep.

For special focus:

1. Study the attributes of God.
2. Study the doctrines of grace.
3. Study the doctrine of sin.
4. Play golf as much as possible.
5. Laugh often, and laugh often at yourself. C.S. Lewis once wrote, "Laughter is a divine gift to the human who is humble. A proud man cannot laugh because he must watch his dignity; he cannot give himself over to the rocking and rolling of his belly. But a poor and happy man laughs heartily because he gives no serious attention to his ego."[94]

Throughout your days and weeks:

1. Identify evidences of grace in others.
2. Encourage and serve others each and every day.
3. Invite and pursue correction.
4. Respond humbly to trials.[95]

Hospitality is the lost virtue among Christians in America today. Of course we are hospitable—not to impress with food or your house—but to serve and love. Christian hospitality doesn't look to gain an advantage but rather is a re-

---

[94] Terry Lindvall, *Surprised by Laughter* (Nashville: Nelson, 1996), 130-31.

[95] Mahaney, *Humility*, 171-72.

sponse to God's overwhelming generosity and welcome.[96] Consider Scripture's teaching on hospitality:

> Romans 12:13: *"Contribute to the needs of the saints and seek to show hospitality."*

> Hebrews 13:1-2: *"Let brotherly love continue. Do not neglect to show hospitality to strangers, for thereby some have entertained angels unawares."*

> 1 Peter 4:7-9: *"The end of all things is at hand; therefore be self-controlled and sober-minded for the sake of your prayers. Above all, keep loving one another earnestly, since love covers a multitude of sins. Show hospitality to one another without grumbling."*

When is the last time you had a brother or sister over for dinner? Has it been a month? Three? Six? Strive to improve in this area of your Christian walk. Meals provide a vital setting for sharing our lives together. Graham Tomlin writes, "When we enter a person's home, we learn much more about them than if we meet elsewhere, because homes reveal a great deal. Visiting a friend's home will tell me a lot about their taste in colors, music, and décor, how they like to arrange their own private world, and what their true values are. We might say blithely in church that we aim to live simply. Whether we really do or not will be quickly revealed by a glance at the way we decorate our homes and manage our possessions. Outside our homes it is easy to pretend, to hide. Inside, all is revealed.... All three, themselves gifts from God, point away from ourselves and outward: faith, toward God and his action in Jesus Christ;

---

[96] Christine D. Pohl, "Hospitality," in *Ancient Faith for the Church's Future,* ed. Mark Husbands and Jeffrey P. Greenman (Downers Grove, IL: IVP Academic, 2008), 150. See Tim Chester, *A Meal With Jesus* (Wheaton, IL: Crossway, 2011).

hope, toward God's future; love, toward both God and our neighbor."[97]

---

[97] Tomlin, *Spiritual Fitness*, 144.

Chapter 8:

Simplicity

The virtue of simplicity is especially important in America.[98] Our culture is very consumeristic so it is worth taking some time to work through this virtue. To begin, it is worth quoting Randy Alcorn at length:

> When it comes to money and possessions, the Bible is sometimes extreme, and occasionally shocking. It turns people away, interferes with our lives, and makes us feel guilty. To avoid guilt feelings, we invent fancy interpretations that get around plain meanings. We come to the Bible wanting comfort, not assaults against our worldview. The church should concern itself with what's spiritual and heavenly. Let *God* talk about love and grace and brotherhood, thank you. Let *us* talk about money and possessions—then do with them whatever we please. Some believers ask each other tough questions: "How are you doing in your marriage? How much time have you been spending in the Word? Sharing your faith? Guarding your sexual purity?" Yet how often do we ask, "Are you winning the battle against materialism?" Or, "Are you cutting your spending and increasing your giving?" Or, "Have you been peeking at those tempting magazines and Internet sites? You know, the ones that entice you to greed?" Financial stewardship seems to be the last bastion of accountability. People are more open about their sexual struggles than battling materialism. Some churches are taking about getting out of debt. I applaud that. But you can be out of debt and still be stingy

---

[98] Every American is rich. Visit globalrichlist.com and enter your income. If you made $50,000 last year, you are in the top 1% of the world's wealthiest people.

and greedy. We don't need to become smarter materialists; we need to repent of materialism. When it comes to stewardship, money management, and giving, most churches operate under a "don't ask, don't tell" policy. We lack communication, accountability, or modeling. It's as if we have an unspoken agreement—"I won't talk about it if you won't." That way we can go on living guilt-free.[99]

Preachers have a bad reputation when it comes to preaching on money all of the time. Doubtless, there are several so-called "pastors" who exploit their people for money. But faithful pastors should not allow the frauds to keep him from Scripture's teaching on the subject. If pastors are faithful expositors, they will be preaching and teaching about money frequently since the Bible frequently mentions this touchy topic. Jesus spoke more about money than he did any other subject except the kingdom of God. Twenty-five percent of his teaching has to do with money and possessions.[100]

Faithful pastors in America should also be teaching about money and possessions frequently because consumerism is the primary "religion" of America. It is the air we breathe, and many of our people do not even realize it. John's words of warning are every bit as relevant today as they were in his context: "Do not love the world or anything in the world. If anyone loves the world, love for the Father is not in them. For everything in the world—the lust of the flesh, the lust of the eyes, and the pride of life—comes not from the Father but from the world. The world and its desires

---

[99] Randy Alcorn, "Dethroning Money to Treasure Christ Above All" in *For the Fame of God's Name*, ed. Sam Storms and Justin Taylor (Wheaton, IL: Crossway, 2010), 308-09.

[100] Camp, *Mere Discipleship*, 172.

pass away, but whoever does the will of God lives forever (1 John 2:15-17 NIV). The lust of the flesh, the lust of the eyes, and the pride of life have to do with material possessions. The word for "life" (*bios*) in 2:16 is often used of "stuff" (Mark 12:44, Luke 8:43, 15:12, 21:4). In 1 John 3:17, the same word is translated "material possessions." In 1 John 5:19, we read that "the whole world lies in the power of the evil one." Sometimes people think that America doesn't have to worry about spiritual warfare. That kind of thing happens "over there." They think that is only needed in more "primitive" cultures. That is exactly what the powers and principalities want you to think. They don't want you to know that they are alive and active, but in reality, many are in bondage. We call it debt. Satan calls it greed. It is one of his many methods (*methodeias*—Eph. 6:11).

What is the most powerful prophet of this religion? Advertising. One author writes, "We're conditioned to feel as though we never have enough. The average American watches over 20,000 commercials each year, and almost every single one of them is designed to convince us we need whatever's being sold. For all of its economic advantages, capitalism thrives on people remaining discontented with what they have. If the American population as a whole ever adhered to Paul's instruction to be content with what we already have (1 Tim. 6:8-9), our economy would collapse overnight.... The truth is that the perpetual hunger for more that fuels capitalism is a form of demonic bondage."[101]

---

[101] Boyd, *The Myth of a Christian Religion*, 133. Ron Sider writes, "We must also dethrone mammon. I fear that many—probably most—Western Christians worship the god of materialism. If their behavior is any measure, they care more about accumulating things than obeying God. How else can we explain the fact that Christians living

On average, people watch 3500 desire-inducing advertisements each day in America. Rodney Clapp writes, "The consumer is schooled in insatiability. He or she is never to be satisfied—at least not for long. The consumer is tutored that people basically consist of unmet needs that can be appeased by commodified goods and experiences."[102]

We are bombarded with advertisements everywhere. Advertisements no longer inform us about the goods being sold but offer an alternate vision of life. All the ingredients for a revival are present: You have the hell – being fat, unpopular, defeated, bored, sad, etc.; you have the salvation – the product; then you have the testimonies – "You can experience this salvation also! Just purchase this product with three installments of $29.99."[103]

---

in the richest nation in human history give less and less to the church even though their annual incomes have increased substantially over the last three decades? Surely biblical people would have joyfully given progressively higher percentages of their income to evangelism and social ministry as they moved from unheard of wealth in terms of all earlier periods of history to even greater, more astounding levels of material abundance. Instead, we have doubled the size of our already spacious houses and the capacity of our garages while reducing the percentage of our giving. Long ago, Jesus said, 'Where your treasure is, there your heart will be also' (Matt. 6:21). And evangelicals are piling up ever-greater treasures in their huge houses, growing vacation homes, and expanding investments," in *The Scandal of the Evangelical Conscience* (Grand Rapids: Baker, 2005), 117.

[102] Rodney Clapp, "Why the Devil Takes VISA," *Christianity Today,* October 7, 1996, quoted in Skye Jethani, *The Divine Commodity* (Grand Rapids: Eerdmans, 2009), 108.

[103] Wells, *Losing our Virtue,* 112-13.

Statistics across the board say that the average American only gives 2.5% of his income.[104] In 2002, Barna did a study and discovered that only 6 percent of so-called born again adults tithed.[105] In the old covenant, the Israelites were commanded to tithe (their tithe being more like 23.5%). New covenant Christians are not commanded to tithe, but should not our standard be higher? The old covenant people of God were largely disobedient and idolatrous. The new covenant people of God have the Holy Spirit! Should not we be eager to give much more? I agree with Randy Alcorn that tithing should be the training wheels of Christian giving. If you are currently giving less, 10% would be a good place to start. Remember, 100% of it is God's—not yours. We are *stewards*, not owners in this world.

Now let's walk through the Scriptures and look at some key passages on money and possessions:

Matthew 6:19-24—*"Do not lay up for yourselves treasures on earth, where moth and rust destroy and where thieves break in and steal, but lay up for yourselves treasures in heaven, where neither moth nor rust destroys and where thieves do not break in and steal. For where your treasure is, there your heart will be also. The eye is the lamp of the body. So, if your eye is healthy, your whole body will be full of light, but if your eye is bad, your whole body will be full of darkness. If then the light in you is darkness, how great is the darkness! No one can serve two masters, for either he will hate the one and love the other, or he will be devoted to the one and despise the other. You cannot serve God and money."*

This is a remarkable truth. What we do with our money and possessions determines where our heart is. Jesus is say-

---

[104] David Platt, *Radical Together* (Colorado Springs: Multnomah, 2011), 16.

[105] Sider, *The Scandal of the Evangelical Conscience*, 21.

ing, show me your checkbook and credit card statement, and I will show you where your heart is. What we do with our money determines what we value. If you say that you wish you had more of a heart for missions, for the unborn, for the poor, for my church—then start giving to those causes. Jesus says your heart will follow. If your money goes to *your* house, *your* toys, *your* hobbies, *your* investments, *your* retirement, *your* family, then your heart will follow it. You can redirect your heart by redirecting your funds.[106] Let's strive to avoid shortsightedness and store up treasures that will last.

> Matthew 19:23-25 — *"And Jesus said to his disciples, 'Truly, I say to you, only with difficulty will a rich person enter the kingdom of heaven. Again I tell you, it is easier for a camel to go through the eye of a needle than for a rich person to enter the kingdom of God.' When the disciples heard this, they were greatly astonished, saying, 'Who then can be saved'?"*

You may have heard a preacher or two try to say that there was a short gate called "the eye of the needle" in the Jerusalem wall that camels could go through, but with difficulty. Unfortunately there is no historical evidence to support this legend.

> Luke 3:10-14 — *"And the crowds asked him, 'What then shall we do?' And he answered them, 'Whoever has two tunics is to share with him who has none, and whoever has food is to do likewise.' Tax collectors also came to be baptized and said to him, 'Teacher, what shall we do?' And he said to them, 'Collect no more than you are authorized to do.' Soldiers also asked him, 'And we, what shall we do?' And he said to them, 'Do not extort money from anyone by threats or by false accusation, and be content with your wages.'*

---

[106] Alcorn, "Dethroning Money to Treasure Christ Above All," 324-25.

Here we have a very interesting passage. Notice how John answers the crowd. Or better, notice how he does not answer. He doesn't say, "pray this prayer," "sign this card," "accept Jesus," but "share your possessions."

Luke 6:20—*"And he lifted up his eyes on his disciples, and said: 'Blessed are you who are poor, for yours is the kingdom of God.'"*

Luke 6:25—*"Woe to you who are full now, for you shall be hungry. Woe to you who laugh now, for you shall mourn and weep."*

Luke 12:15—*"And he said to them, 'Take care, and be on your guard against all covetousness, for one's life does not consist in the abundance of his possessions.'"*

Evaluate your life right now. Would an objective outside observer conclude that your life does consist in the abundance of possessions? The default American mindset is directly opposed to the mindset of Jesus. We tend to think "better job, bigger house, nicer car, more exotic vacations," and on and on.

Luke 14:33—*"So therefore, any one of you who does not renounce all that he has cannot be my disciple."*

What does this mean for you? How can you seek to apply this radical demand?

Acts 2:44-45—*"And all who believed were together and had all things in common. And they were selling their possessions and belongings and distributing the proceeds to all, as any had need."*

Acts 4:32-35—*"Now the full number of those who believed were of one heart and soul, and no one said that any of the things that belonged to him was his own, but they had everything in common. And with great power the apostles were giving their testimony to the resurrection of the Lord Jesus, and great grace was upon them all. There was not a needy person among them, for as many as were owners of lands or houses sold them and brought the proceeds of what was sold and laid it at the apostles' feet, and it was distributed to each as any had need."*

Does your church life resemble the Bible in the least bit when it comes to possessions? What can you do to correct this? Initiate.

Acts 20:35— *"It is more blessed to give than to receive."*

Do you believe this?

Romans 13:8—*"Owe no one nothing"* (my trans. of *medeni meden opheilete*).

Is it okay to go in debt? I think it is okay to go in debt in rare scenarios. Perhaps it is justifiable with college, vehicles, and homes, but too often Christians do not even give this verse a second thought. "Surely it doesn't mean what it sounds like it means."

2 Corinthians 8:7-9— *"But as you excel in everything—in faith, in speech, in knowledge, in all earnestness, and in our love for you— see that you excel in this act of grace also. I say this not as a command, but to prove by the earnestness of others that your love also is genuine. For you know the grace of our Lord Jesus Christ, that though he was rich, yet for your sake he became poor, so that you by his poverty might become rich."*

"Grace-giving" can end up meaning give what you feel like. But we usually do not feel like giving. For example, 40% of "born again Christians" give nothing. Again, it is *my opinion* that Paul would expect those transformed by Jesus and his Spirit to be giving more in the new covenant than was required in the old covenant.

2 Corinthians 9:11— *"You will be enriched in every way to be generous in every way, which through us will produce thanksgiving to God."*

It is important to clarify that making money is not a bad thing in itself. Pursuing raises and promotions is not either, as long as you are not doing it to raise your standard of living. It is fine to own things so long as they do not own you. We should seek to make more money so we can raise our standard of giving. Giving naturally follows grace. Statistics on giving indicate that the average evangelical household has not experienced grace.

Galatians 6:6-10—*"One who is taught the word must share all good things with the one who teaches. Do not be deceived: God is not mocked, for whatever one sows, that will he also reap. For the one who sows to his own flesh will from the flesh reap corruption, but the one who sows to the Spirit will from the Spirit reap eternal life. And let us not grow weary of doing good, for in due season we will reap, if we do not give up. So then, as we have opportunity, let us do good to everyone, and especially to those who are of the household of faith."*

In this shocking passage, Paul says that how we share our possessions will in part determine where we spend our eternity.

Philippians 4:10-13—*"I rejoiced greatly in the Lord that at last you renewed your concern for me. Indeed, you were concerned, but you had no opportunity to show it. I am not saying this because I am in need, for I have learned to be content whatever the circumstances. I know what it is to be in need, and I know what it is to have plenty. I have learned the secret of being content in any and every situation, whether well fed or hungry, whether living in plenty or in want. I can do all this through him who gives me strength."* (NIV)

1 John 3:16-17—*"By this we know love, that he laid down his life for us, and we ought to lay down our lives for the brothers. But if anyone has the world's goods and sees his brother in need, yet closes his heart against him, how does God's love abide in him?"*

For John, love must not remain in the abstract. John's letters are *full* of exhortations to love one another, and interestingly, this is the only place where John gives a specific example: sharing possessions!

Colossians 3:5—*"...greed, which is idolatry"* (NIV)

Both Colossians 3:5 and Ephesians 5:5 say that greed is idolatry. This is yet another devastating statement. Randy Alcorn writes, "Mall window shoppers and catalog browsers should remind themselves that greed isn't a harmless pastime; it's a serious offense against God. Just as one who lusts is an adulterer (Matt. 5:28), and one who hates is a murderer (1 John 3:15), one who is greedy is an idolater (Col. 3:5). No sin is greater than worshiping false gods and thereby depreciating the only true God. The fact that idol worshipers may surround us doesn't reduce the seriousness of our offense. Greed violates the first commandment: 'I am the LORD your God... You shall have no other gods before me' (Ex. 20:2-3). The eight commandment prohibits stealing (Ex. 20:15), a product of greed. The tenth commandment forbids covetousness (Ex. 20:17). Remarkably, the ten great laws of God, written in stone, contain no fewer than three prohibitions against materialism."[107]

1 Timothy 6:6-10—*"Now there is great gain in godliness with contentment, for we brought nothing into the world, and we cannot take anything out of the world. But if we have food and clothing, with these we will be content. But those who desire to be rich fall into temptation, into a snare, into many senseless and harmful desires that plunge people into ruin and destruction. For the love of money is a root of all kinds of evils. It is through this craving that some have wandered away from the faith and pierced themselves with many pangs."*

Hebrews 13:5-6—*"Keep your life free from love of money, and be content with what you have, for he has said, 'I will never leave you nor forsake you.' So we can confidently say, 'The Lord is my helper; I will not fear; what can man do to me?'"*

---

[107] Randy Alcorn, "Dethroning Money to Treasure Christ Above All," 315.

These passages should give us a good sense of the biblical attitude we should seek to have towards money and possessions. The early church fathers adopted the same mindset. The following quote summarizes the early church fathers: "To accumulate wealth is to pervert it, not only because real wealth must always be moving and active, but also because the purpose of wealth is to meet human need.... This line of argument repeatedly leads the authors to conclude that the intended use of wealth is the common good. Private property is justifiable only to the extent it is used for sharing, to promote the equality that the present order does not foster."[108]

Giving forms our hearts and lives; it is an active way to root out greed. It shows the world who our God is. As N.T. Wright puts it, "The habit of giving, of giving generously, is not an extra option for keen Christians. It is absolutely obligatory on all—because our whole calling is to reflect God the creator, and the main thing we know about this true God is that his very nature is self-giving, generous love. The reason why 'God loves a cheerful giver' (2 Corinthians 9:7) is that that's what God himself is like."[109]

Randy Alcorn writes, "Five minutes after we die, it will be too late to go back and redo our lives. Gazing into the eyes of the Christ we treasure, we'll know exactly how we should have lived. God has given us his Word so we don't have to wait to die to find out how we should have lived. And he's given us his Spirit to empower us to live that way now. Ask yourself: Five minutes after I die, what will I wish

---

[108] Justo Gonzalez, *Faith and Wealth* (Eugene, OR: Wipf and Stock, 2002), 229.

[109] Wright, *After You Believe*, 282.

I would have done with the money and possessions God entrusted to my care? What will I wish I'd given away while I still had the chance? When you've come up with an answer, why not do it now? Why shouldn't we spend the rest of our lives closing the gap between what we are doing and what we'll wish we would have done for his glory?"[110] Read obituaries. Yours is coming. Visit cemeteries. Your body will soon lie in one. Visit junkyards. Your stuff will end up there. Spend with the judgment seat in mind! Regarding your use of money and possessions, will he say, "Well done, my good and faithful servant"?

---

[110] Alcorn, "Dethroning Money to Treasure Christ Above All," 327.

PART II

CRUCIFORM LOVE

In Part II, we will seek to understand and apply six key passages that help us understand the primary Christian virtue: love.

Chapter 9:

Cruciform Love: Philippians 2:1-11

Do you have a Jesus mindset? Another way to ask this is, are you a loving person? Or are you a Christ-like person? The content of this theme can be summed up by 1 John 4:10-11, which reads, "In this is love, not that we have loved God but that he loved us and sent his Son to be the propitiation for our sins. Beloved, if God so loved us, we also ought to love one another."

God has loved us in and through Jesus, and we are called to imitate his loving action. We will see that in the cross of Christ, we find both the provision for salvation as well as the pattern for life. We find the source of salvation and well as the shape of Christian living. We find the power to live a new life and the paradigm for how to live it.[111]

New Testament scholar Michael Gorman has called Philippians 2 Paul's "master story."[112] This is love according to Paul. It is what he elsewhere calls the "law" of the Messiah (Gal. 6:2).

We do not know a lot about the situation in Philippi, but from the content of the letter, we do know there was disuni-

---

[111] I owe this terminology to Michael Gorman.

[112] Michael Gorman, *Cruciformity* (Grand Rapids: Eerdmans, 2001), 88, 215. Earlier, he writes, "For Paul, to be in Christ is to be a living exegesis of this narrative of Christ, a new performance of the original drama of exaltation following humiliation, of humiliation as the voluntary renunciation of rights and selfish gain in order to serve and obey," 92.

ty. We are not sure why, but Paul calls them to unity in love. We also know they were suffering (Phil. 1:29). The passage reads:

> So if there is any encouragement in Christ, any comfort from love, any participation in the Spirit, any affection and sympathy, ² complete my joy by being of the same mind, having the same love, being in full accord and of one mind. ³ Do nothing from rivalry or conceit, but in humility count others more significant than yourselves. ⁴ Let each of you look not only to his own interests, but also to the interests of others. ⁵ Have this mind among yourselves, which is yours in Christ Jesus, ⁶ who, though he was in the form of God, did not count equality with God a thing to be grasped, ⁷ but made himself nothing, taking the form of a servant, being born in the likeness of men. ⁸ And being found in human form, he humbled himself by becoming obedient to the point of death, even death on a cross. ⁹ Therefore God has highly exalted him and bestowed on him the name that is above every name, ¹⁰ so that at the name of Jesus every knee should bow, in heaven and on earth and under the earth, ¹¹ and every tongue confess that Jesus Christ is Lord, to the glory of God the Father.

This passage breaks down easily into three parts: exhortation (1-5), example (5-8), exaltation (9-11). First, an examination of the exhortation. Verses 1-2 are the basis of the exhortation. Paul writes, "So if there is any encouragement in Christ, any comfort from love, any participation in the Spirit, any affection and sympathy, complete my joy by being of the same mind, having the same love, being in full accord and of one mind." In other words, "If you are a believer, make my joy complete." Verse 2 contains the *concern* of the exhortation: unity in love. Notice the emphasis on unity: like-minded, same love, one in spirit, of one mind.

Verses 3-4 contain the *content* of the exhortation. Paul lists those things that war against unity. Selfish ambition is self-seeking, rivalry, self-interest, and self-centeredness. Vain conceit is a vain or exaggerated self-evaluation, vanity, conceit, vain pride.[113] Is not all pride vain? Paul is simply saying do nothing out of selfishness. Do nothing when only thinking about you. Rather, in humility, value others above yourselves. In other words, be selfless.

Paul is simply calling us to selfless living here. How can we seek to eradicate selfish ambition and vain conceit from our community? In his classic book, *Life Together*, Dietrich Bonhoeffer supplies seven principles for us. Christians should:

- Hold their tongues, refusing to speak uncharitably about a Christian brother or sister;
- Cultivate the humility that comes from understanding that they, like Paul, are the greatest of sinners and can only live in God's sight by his grace;
- Listen "long and patiently" so that they will understand their fellow Christian's need;
- Refuse to consider their time and calling so valuable that they cannot be interrupted to help with unexpected needs, no matter how small or menial;
- Bear the burden of their brothers and sisters in the Lord, both by preserving their freedom and by forgiving their sinful abuse of that freedom;
- Declare God's word to their fellow believers when they need to hear it;
- Understand that Christian authority is characterized by service and does not call attention to the person who performs the service.[114]

---

[113] For you Greek readers, notice the word plays in 2:3-11: *Kenodoxian* and *ekenōsen* and *Kenodoxian* and *doxan*.

[114] Dietrich Bonhoeffer, *Life Together* (New York: HarperOne, 1954), 90-109, quoted in Frank Thielman, *Philippians* (Grand Rapids: Zondervan, 1995), 107.

We can also eradicate selfish ambition and vain conceit by looking at the perfect example of selfless living, which leads us to our next consideration: the example given in verses 5b-8. Paul has given the exhortation; now he wants to motivate his readers by pointing to the One who truly lived selflessly. Jesus is our "how to" manual. So much for Horton's theory that one does not need Jesus for a better morality.[115] We are to fulfill the pattern of the Messiah. We are to behave "incarnationally." We are to adopt the Jesus mindset. So what is the Jesus mindset?

From the passage, we see that the mind is very important. Verse two exhorts us to be like-minded (*auto phronēte*) and to be of one mind (*hen phronountes*), while verse five exhorts us to have the same mindset (*phroneite*) as Christ. True love begins by right thinking. We must adopt the same selfless mindset that Jesus had.

Most scholars see verses 6-11 as an early Christian hymn. This provides us with a glimpse of early Christian thought and worship. The phrase, "a thing to be grasped" is probably better translated as "something to be used to his own advantage" (NIV), as there is growing consensus in New Testament scholarship that the word (*harpagmos*) has the idea of using something for one's own advantage (NIV, NRSV, HCSB). There is probably an allusion to Adam in these verses. The phrase "in the form of God" (*en morphē theou*) has some correspondence to "the image of God" (*eikona theou*) in Genesis 1:27. Adam, in arrogance, sought to be like God, but the last Adam, in humility, became human.

Historically, there has been a lot of controversy surrounding verse 7, particularly with the verb "emptied him-

---

[115] Horton, *Christless Christianity*, 94.

self" or "made himself nothing" (NIV) (*ekenōsen*). He did not literally empty himself of anything. In fact, he added something. How did he make himself nothing? The text tells us: By adding a human nature and dying on the cross. Donald McLeod writes, "The theological starting-point must be that Christ already had an equality with God (*isa to theo*). As such, he had rights: to be recognized; to be revered; to be served by angels; to be immune from poverty, pain and humiliation. Had he been motivated by vainglory, he would have insisted on such rights. Instead, he did not regard them as something to be clung to (*harpagmos*). He could have rejected the proposal that he become servant; or, he could, while consenting to be sent forth, have insisted that it should be in a manner consistent with his dignity. He could have insisted on coming, not *incognito*, but in the full blaze of divine paraphernalia and insignia: as Yahweh came on Mount Sinai (Ex.19:16ff.); or as he himself would one day come in the glory of the *parousia;* or as the Tempter suggested in the desert, immune to weakness, renowned as a potentate, guarded by angels; or at least in the glory he enjoyed momentarily on the Mount of Transfiguration, receiving from God the Father honour and acclamation (2 Pet. 1:17). These were his rights, but, being in the form of God, he did not insist on these rights."[116]

Paul is saying that the story of Christ must become the story of the community.[117] Notice how verses 3-4 are parallel to 6-8. Both have a negative, then a "but," then a positive. We could paraphrase it this way: "Do not be selfish, rather

---

[116] Donald Macleod, *The Person of Christ* (Downers Grove, IL: IVP, 1998), 214.

[117] Luke Timothy Johnson, *Living Jesus* (New York: HarperOne, 1999), 114.

be selfless because Jesus was not selfish, rather he was self-less."

Michael Gorman is right to call this chapter, Paul's "master story." Notice the pattern, the "law" of the Messiah in the following verses:

Ephesians 5:1-2— *"Therefore be imitators of God, as beloved children.* ² *And walk in love, as Christ loved us and gave himself up for us, a fragrant offering and sacrifice to God."*

John 13:14-15— *"If I then, your Lord and Teacher, have washed your feet, you also ought to wash one another's feet.* ¹⁵ *For I have given you an example, that you also should do just as I have done to you."*

John 13:34-35— *"A new commandment I give to you, that you love one another: just as I have loved you, you also are to love one another.* ³⁵ *By this all people will know that you are my disciples, if you have love for one another."*

Romans 15:2-3— *"Let each of us please his neighbor for his good, to build him up.* ³ *For Christ did not please himself."*

1 Corinthians 10:32-11:1— *"Give no offense to Jews or to Greeks or to the church of God, just as I try to please everyone in everything I do, not seeking my own advantage, but that of many, that they may be saved. Be imitators of me, as I am of Christ."*

2 Corinthians 8:9— *"For you know the grace of our Lord Jesus Christ, that though he was rich, yet for your sake he became poor, so that you by his poverty might become rich."*

Notice the similarities of this last verse with Philippians 2. The phrase "though he was rich" is parallel to "though he was in the form of God," while "for your sake he became poor" is similar to "he emptied himself" and "he humbled himself." It is self sacrifice for the sake of others. Yet for your sake! Jesus refrains from any acts of selfishness or self interest but rather acts for the benefit of others. God gives of himself for the good of others, and the people of

God are to follow suit. Cruciform love is two-dimensional: it does not seek its own interest, but seeks the interest of others.[118]

God's love expresses itself in self-sacrifice, and specifically, there are two steps of self-denial: becoming human and dying on a cross. Crucifixion was reserved by the Romans for insurrectionists (those who rebel against Roman rule) or recalcitrant slaves. Only for high treason could a Roman citizen be crucified. That is why Paul says the message of a crucified Messiah is a stumbling block to Jews and foolishness to Greeks (1 Cor. 1:23).

God on a cross! The second person of the Trinity was beaten, flogged, nailed to a cross, muscles cramping, and between cramps, he had to pull himself up for a breath. He would have had searing pain where tissue that was torn from his lacerated back rubbed against the rough timber as he moved up and down to breath. He experienced severe blood loss and dehydration; decreased oxygen and increased carbon dioxide caused acidic conditions in the tissues. Fluid built up in the lungs. He suffocated. His heart stopped. He died. There would have been no cross necklaces or tattoos in Philippi.

It was excruciating (Latin, *excruciatus*, or "out of the cross"). Cicero described crucifixion as "a most cruel and disgusting punishment" and suggested that "the very mention of the cross should be far removed not only from a Roman citizen's body, but from his mind, his eyes, his ears."

He did this for us, willingly. Christian, be amazed. But why does Paul bring this up here? He is holding up Jesus as an example of selfless living. He is grounding his exhorta-

---

[118] Gorman, *Cruciformity,* 170.

tion in the example of Jesus. Fathers, mothers, husbands, wives, siblings, employees, is this your posture towards each other? Jesus had certain rights. He did not take advantage of them but renounced them for the good of others. We must do the same. Christians give, not get. Like our Lord, we serve, not be served.

Finally, in verses 9-11, Paul describes the exaltation of Jesus. In the midst of suffering, Paul reminds them who they are and whose they are. This is a word of comfort. He tells us that it is Jesus who is the world's true Lord. He explains the significance of his name: it is *given* to him by the Father; it is in fact the name above every name, meaning the divine name *YHWH*; it means that Jesus can and will be given the devotion due God alone.[119]

The title "Lord" in the LXX (Greek Old Testament) was *YHWH*. This way Paul could show his equality with God the Father, yet he refrains from calling Jesus *YHWH*, which is reserved for the Father. Notice how thoroughly Trinitarian these passages are:

2:1—*So if there is any encouragement in Christ* [God the Son]

2:1—*Any comfort from* [his] *love* [God the Son]

2:1—*Any participation in the Spirit* [Holy Spirit]

2:6—*Who,* [God the Son], *though he was in the form of God* [God the Father]

2:9—*Therefore God [God the Father] has highly exalted him* [God the Son]

2:11—*And every tongue confess that Jesus Christ* [God the Son] *is Lord, to the glory of God the Father [God the Father]*

Here Paul quotes one of the most powerful passages in Scripture claiming that *YHWH* alone is God. God is saying

---

[119] Gorman, *Reading Paul*, 103.

that Israel's opponents will be put to shame. Isaiah 45:20-24 says,

> *Assemble yourselves and come; draw near together, you survivors of the nations! They have no knowledge who carry about their wooden idols, and keep on praying to a god that cannot save. Declare and present your case; let them take counsel together! Who told this long ago? Who declared it of old? Was it not I, the LORD? And there is no other god besides me, a righteous God and a Savior; there is none besides me. "Turn to me and be saved, all the ends of the earth! For I am God, and there is no other. By myself I have sworn; from my mouth has gone out in righteousness a word that shall not return: 'To me every knee shall bow, every tongue shall swear allegiance.'"Only in the LORD, it shall be said of me, are righteousness and strength; to him shall come and be ashamed all who were incensed against him.*

For those familiar with the Hebrew Scriptures, this would be a grand statement! Paul applies this passage about the exclusivity of *YHWH* to Jesus. But for those whose background was more Roman than Hebrew, they would hear another message. Claiborne and Haw write, "So many of the words we just throw around in Christian circles today were loaded with political meaning for Jesus and his contemporaries. Many were words Jesus swiped from the imperial lexicon and spun on their heads in beautiful political satire."[120]

For example, "gospel" (*euangelion*) meant an imperial pronouncement that an heir to the empire's throne had been born or that a distant battle had been won. When an important battle was won, they would send out messengers to

---

[120] Shane Claiborne and Chris Haw, *Jesus for President* (Grand Rapids: Zondervan, 2008), 66. I am dependent on this book for the following paragraph. See also Gorman, *Cruciformity*, 353.

announce this gospel. Caesar Augustus (27 BC—AD 14) articulated his gospel in the following inscription found in Myra: 'Divine Augustus Caesar, son of god, imperator of land and sea, the benefactor and savior of the whole world, has brought you peace." Or consider this inscription from 9 BC:

> The providence which has ordered the whole of our life, showing concern and zeal, has ordained the most perfect consummation for human life by giving to it Augustus, by filling him with virtue for doing the work of a benefactor among men, and by sending in him, as it were, a savior for us and those who come after us, to make war to cease, to create order everywhere... [S]ince the Caesar [Augustus] through his appearance has exceeded the hopes of all former good messages [*euangelia*], surpassing not only the benefactors who came before him, but also leaving no hope that anyone in the future would surpass him, and since for the world the birthday of the god was the beginning of his good messages [*euangelia*].[121]

"Son of God" was a popular title for kings and emperors. Alexander the Great took that title as well as king of kings. Augustus declared that Julius Caesar (his adopted father) had become a god after his murder. Most subsequent emperors similarly divinized their predecessors. The new emperor would then claim the title "son of god."[122] "Savior" was used of Caesar Augustus when he healed the chaos of Rome and brought it into a new golden age.

"Lord" was used of rulers, but particularly of the supreme ruler. The pledge of allegiance in the Roman Empire was *Caesar ho kurios*—Caesar is Lord. What was the funda-

---

[121] Priene inscription quoted in Michael Gorman, *Reading Paul* (Eugene, OR: Cascade, 2008), 43-44.

[122] N.T. Wright, *Paul* (Minneapolis: Fortress, 2009), 64.

mental confession of the early church? *Jesus* is Lord. The first Christians were showing where their true allegiance was. It was also making a statement about who truly rules the world. If Jesus is Lord, Caesar is not (hence, persecution). Acts 17:7-8 reads, "They are all acting against the decrees of Caesar, saying that there is another king, Jesus. And the people and the city authorities were disturbed when they heard these things."

So Rome had a savior, a gospel, and a lord, and Paul wants the Philippians to know that those causing suffering say that Caesar is Lord but they and their lord will join with all others to declare that the true Lord is none other than the Jesus whom the Romans crucified.

Philippi was a Roman colony. As such, if trouble came, they could call on the emperor from the mother city to come rescue them. As savior and lord, he had the power to impose his will on the whole known world.[123] In Philippians 3:20, Paul writes, "But our citizenship is in heaven, and from it we await a Savior, the Lord Jesus Christ." Their citizenship, their commonwealth (*politeuma*, from *polis*) is not in Rome but in heaven. They are a colony within a colony: a colony of heaven within the colony of Rome.[124]

The church is to be a contrast society. G.B. Caird writes, "Each local church is a colony of heaven, its members enjoying full citizenship of the heavenly city...but charged with the responsibility of bringing the world to acknowledge the sovereignty of Christ."[125] Our city charter is the story of the

---

[123] Ibid., 72.

[124] Gorman, *Cruciformity*, 358.

[125] G.B. Caird, *Paul's Letters from Prison in the Revised Standard Version*, NCB (Oxford: Oxford University Press, 1976), 148.

crucified Christ, and we are called to live as citizens of that city: whatever happens, conduct yourselves as citizens worthy of the gospel of Christ (1:27, my translation of *politeuesthe*).

Michael Gorman summarizes the message of Philippians well:

> Live faithfully now as a colony of citizens of that heavenly imperial city, in the midst of this colony of Rome. Your Lord and Savior—your "Emperor"—is Jesus, whose cruciform pattern of faith, love, power, and hope is the city charter of your colony. And as you live by this charter, do so in unity, for you must be one as you face persecution together for the sake of Christ, just as I, Paul, am imprisoned—though the gospel we sing, preach, and live is not.[126]

Jesus is the true Lord of the world. All will bow and recognize his authority. Believer, do nothing out of selfish ambition or vain conceit, but in humility value others above yourselves and look to their interests, not your own, just like your Lord did. Adopt the Jesus mindset. As Fred Zaspel writes, "Indeed, following our Lord's example, what limits can we possibly set? Is there anything too beneath us if, in doing so, we would help our brothers and sisters? Are we called to give ourselves? What is that when compared to our Lord's condescension—God from the glories of heaven to the shameful cross. Are we called to endure wrongs? Did he not endure more? Must we surrender our rights? Our Lord did not retain his. What possible limits could we set, when we see another in need? Our Lord's condescension was   infinite."[127]

---

[126] Gorman, *Cruciformity*, 359.

[127] Fred Zaspel, "Imitating the Incarnation: B.B. Warfield on Following Christ," *Sound of Grace* 183 (Dec 2011-Jan 2012), 10.

Chapter 10:

Cruciform Love: The Pattern of the Messiah (Galatians 6:2)

Before examining the passage, it is always helpful to ask, "Where are we in the story?" God created the earth and all that was in it. Adam and Eve rebelled against his rule, and the world has never been the same because of it. God graciously called a pagan named Abram and promised to bless him with land and offspring, and he and his family would in turn bless the nations. His family (Israel) was unfaithful from the start. God promised them that their king, David, would have a Son whose throne would be eternal. He also promised a new covenant where the people would be faithful, and his people would not be limited to Israel alone but would include the nations. Jesus died and rose again and poured out the Spirit. The church begins to spread. The apostle Paul plants a church in Galatia, but false teachers come in. They are trying to say that the old covenant is still in force. They are trying to make the Gentile Galatians obey the Jewish law. So Paul writes to sort it all out.

One of the reasons why returning to the law was attractive to the Galatians was because it gave very specific details on how to live in everyday life. The law is full of ethical prescription. They must have been a tad uncomfortable with the freedom of the new age. This is why Paul says, "For freedom Christ has set us free; stand firm therefore, and do not submit again to a yoke of slavery" (Gal. 5:1). In chapters 5 and 6, Paul wants to show them that the Spirit and the example of Christ are sufficient as a guide to life. In these chapters, he lays out what behavior in God's new world should look like.

It will be helpful to look at Galatians 5:13-6:2 to get a feel for the context of 6:2, where our focus will be. I will be making a case for a certain understanding of the phrase "law of the Messiah." So walk with me as we think Paul's thoughts after him:

> *For you were called to freedom, brothers. Only do not use your freedom as an opportunity for the flesh, but through love serve one another. For the whole law is fulfilled in one word: "You shall love your neighbor as yourself." But if you bite and devour one another, watch out that you are not consumed by one another. But I say, walk by the Spirit, and you will not gratify the desires of the flesh. For the desires of the flesh are against the Spirit, and the desires of the Spirit are against the flesh, for these are opposed to each other, to keep you from doing the things you want to do. But if you are led by the Spirit, you are not under the law. Now the works of the flesh are evident: sexual immorality, impurity, sensuality, idolatry, sorcery, enmity, strife, jealousy, fits of anger, rivalries, dissensions, divisions, envy, drunkenness, orgies, and things like these. I warn you, as I warned you before, that those who do such things will not inherit the kingdom of God. But the fruit of the Spirit is love, joy, peace, patience, kindness, goodness, faithfulness, gentleness, self-control; against such things there is no law. And those who belong to Christ Jesus have crucified the flesh with its passions and desires. If we live by the Spirit, let us also walk by the Spirit. Let us not become conceited, provoking one another, envying one another. Brothers, if anyone is caught in any transgression, you who are spiritual should restore him in a spirit of gentleness. Keep watch on yourself, lest you too be tempted. Bear one another's burdens, and so fulfill the law of Christ.*

What is the law of the Messiah?[128] There are really two main options: it is the law of Moses, or it is something different. Virtually all of the 30 preceding uses of "law" in Galatians refer to the Mosaic law.[129] This being the case, we must have a good reason to say this is *not* a reference to the Mosaic law, and we do; here are three reasons.[130]

First, all the negative references to the law in Galatians:

2:16—"*a person is not justified by the works of the law, but through faith in Jesus Christ*"

2:19—"*through the law I died to the law*"

2:21—"*if righteousness were through the law, then Christ died for no purpose*"

3:2—"*Did you receive the Spirit by the works of the law or by hearing with faith?*"

3:10—"*For all who rely on the works of the law are under a curse*"

3:11—"*Now it is evident that no one is justified before God by the law*"

3:12—"*The law is not of faith*"

3:13—"*Christ redeemed us from the curse of the law*"

3:18—"*For if the inheritance comes by the law, it no longer comes by promise*"

3:21b—"*For if a law had been given that could give life, then righteousness would indeed be by the law*"

---

[128] This chapter comes from my book titled *What is New Covenant Theology? An Introduction* (Frederick, MD: New Covenant Media, 2012).

[129] The references are: 2:16 (3X), 19 (2X), 21, 3:2, 5, 10 (2X), 11, 12, 13, 17, 18, 19, 21 (3X), 23, 24, 4:4, 5, 21 (2X), 5:3, 4, 14, 18, 23, 6:2, 13.

[130] I have been most helped by Richard B. Hays, "Christology and Ethics in Galatians: The Law of Christ," *The Catholic Biblical Quarterly* 49.1 (Jan 1987) in this chapter.

3:23—*"we were held captive under the law, imprisoned until the coming faith would be revealed"*

3:24—*"So then, the law was our guardian until Christ came"*

4:5—*"God sent his Son to redeem those who were under the law"*

5:4—*"You are severed from Christ, you who would be justified by the law"*

5:18—*"But if you are led by the Spirit, you are not under the law"*

5:23—*"Against such things there is no law"*

So far, Christ and the law have been presented as being in sharp opposition.[131] Only here in Galatians 6:2 are the two used together positively. This fact suggests that Paul has some other "law" in mind here.

Second, Paul adds three extremely important words to the word "law": *"of the Messiah"* (*tou Christou*)! Paul has in mind something distinct from the law of Moses here.[132]

Third, 1 Corinthians 9:19-23 shows definitively that the law of Christ is something distinct from the law of Moses. There we read:

> *For though I am free from all, I have made myself a servant to all, that I might win more of them. To the Jews I became as a Jew, in order to win Jews. To those under the law I became as one under the law (though not being myself under the law) that I might win those under the law. To those outside the law I became as one outside the law (not being outside the law of God but under the law of Christ) that I might win those outside the law. To the weak I became weak, that I might win the weak. I have become all things to all people, that*

---

[131] Richard B. Hays, *Galatians, The New Interpreters Bible* (Nashville: Abingdon, 2000), 333.

[132] David G. Horrell, *Solidarity and Difference* (New York: T & T Clark International, 2005), 227.

*by all means I might save some. I do it all for the sake of the gospel,
that I may share with them in its blessings.*

Notice that Paul clearly distinguishes the law of Moses
from the law of God. Then he defines the law of God as being "in-lawed to Messiah" (*ennomos Christou*). In other
words, one fulfills the will of God not by putting oneself
under the law of Moses, but by being under the jurisdiction
of Jesus.

These three points lead me to believe Paul has something
different in mind here, but what is it? He is using an ironic,
rhetorical word-play, like he does with faith "working"
(Gal. 5:6).[133] Throughout the letter, Paul has also contrasted
faith and works, but then towards the end, he says that all
that matters is faith "working." Paul is very clever. This is
not the only time that Paul has used the word "law" meta-
phorically. Consider the following instances:

Galatians 5:23 — *"Against such things there is no law"*

Romans 3:27 — *"Then what becomes of our boasting? It is ex-
cluded. By what kind of law? By a law of works? No, but by the law
of faith."*

Romans 7:23 — *"but I see in my members another law waging
war against the law of my mind and making me captive to the law of
sin that dwells in my members."*

Romans 7:25 — *"Thanks be to God through Jesus Christ our
Lord! So then, I myself serve the law of God with my mind, but with
my flesh I serve the law of sin."*

Romans 8:2 — *"For the law of the Spirit of life has set you free in
Christ Jesus from the law of sin and death."*

It is true that Paul usually has the Mosaic law-covenant
in mind when he uses the word "law" (*nomos*), but not al-

---

[133] Hays, "Christology and Ethics in Galatians: The Law of Christ," 275.

ways. The Galatians want to be under law so Paul grants it. In Galatians 6:2, Paul cleverly coins the phrase "law of the Messiah" to refer to the pattern of the Messiah.[134] What is that pattern?

He has already shown what this pattern is in the letter. Christians are called to carry one another's burdens and in this way fulfill the pattern of the Messiah. Paul has presented Christ as the ultimate burden bearer.[135] His readers would have already seen this in the letter:

> 1:3-4—*"Grace to you and peace from God our Father and the Lord Jesus Christ, who gave himself for our sins to deliver us from the present evil age, according to the will of our God and Father."*

> 2:20—*"And the life I now live in the flesh I live by faith in the Son of God, who loved me and gave himself for me."*

> 3:13—*"Christ redeemed us from the curse of the law by becoming a curse for us."*

> 4:4-5—*"But when the fullness of time had come, God sent forth his Son, born of woman, born under the law, to redeem those who were under the law, so that we might receive adoption as sons."*

Notice the pattern: Jesus gives of himself for the good of others. This is his "law," his pattern. One New Testament scholar paraphrases: "Bear one another's burdens, and in this way you yourselves will repeat Christ's deed, bringing to completion in your communities the law that Christ has already brought to completion in the sentence about loving the neighbor."[136]

---

134 Ibid., 276.

135 Ben Witherington III, *Grace in Galatia* (Grand Rapids: Eerdmans, 1998), 423.

136 J.L. Martyn, *Galatians*, AB 33A (New York: Doubleday, 1997), 547-48.

Therefore, doing justice to the fact that Paul is using a word-play on the word "law" here, a better translation may be "basic principle,"[137] or "regulative principle," or "structure of existence,"[138] or "normative pattern."[139] "Law" could also be translated as "main principle" since this burden-bearing, self-giving love is seen as the essence of what Christ was about.[140] This is the "Torah" of the Messiah. It is his instruction. This is the "way of Jesus." This is the "Jesus mindset." This is cruciform love.

The pattern of the Messiah is fulfilled by a mode of operation that seeks the good of others even at cost to oneself. The story of Jesus must become the story of the community of Jesus. The pattern of Christ's self-sacrificial death on a cross has now become the rule for our experience.[141] As another New Testament scholar puts it, "The pattern of Jesus' character—the way he 'loved me and gave himself for me' (Gal. 2:20b)—is now to be the pattern of the Christian's life."[142]

It is a pattern of self-enslaving love. In Galatians 5:13, he exhorts us to become slaves of one another in love. We use freedom as an opportunity to become slaves of others. We are servants. We put the needs of others above our own. Re-

---

[137] Horrell, *Solidarity and Difference*, 230.

[138] Hays, "Christology and Ethics in Galatians: The Law of Christ," 276, 286.

[139] Horrell, *Solidarity and Difference*, 230.

[140] Witherington, *Grace in Galatia*, 424.

[141] Richard B. Hays, *First Corinthians, Interpretation* (Louisville: John Knox Press: 1997), 154.

[142] Johnson, *Living Jesus*, 46.

call that this is the same statement Paul makes in Philippians 2:3-8:

> *Do nothing from rivalry or conceit, but in humility count others more significant than yourselves. Let each of you look not only to his own interests, but also to the interests of others. Have this mind among yourselves, which is yours in Christ Jesus, who, though he was in the form of God, did not count equality with God a thing to be grasped, but made himself nothing, taking the form of a servant, being born in the likeness of men. And being found in human form, he humbled himself by becoming obedient to the point of death, even death on a cross.*

We are to give of self for the good of others. We put them first, just as Jesus put us first by becoming human and dying on a cross for us. He did not come to be served, but to serve.

From Galatians we learn that this activity also fulfills the law of Moses (Gal. 5:14). Jesus taught the same thing. In Matthew 7:12, he said, "So whatever you wish that others would do to you, do also to them, for this is the Law and the Prophets." In Matthew 22:40, he said "On these two commandments depend all the Law and the Prophets." Paul also teaches that love fulfills the law in Romans 13:8-10. Through the Spirit and the cross, we bring to fruition what the law always pointed to.[143] F.F. Bruce writes, "So far as Paul is concerned, guidance for the church is provided by the law of love, not by the 'law of commandments and or-

---

[143] As Gordon Fee puts it, "The aim of Torah, which Torah was helpless to bring off, was to create a loving community in which God's own character and purposes are fulfilled as God's people love one another the way he loves them.... the Spirit has 'replaced' Torah by fulfilling the aim of Torah," *God's Empowering Presence* (Peabody, MA: Hendrickson, 1994), 426.

dinances' (Ephesians 2:15). In his letters he himself lays down guidelines for his converts and others, often couched in the imperative mood, but these guidelines mostly concern personal relations.... Here if anywhere Luther entered into the mind of Paul: 'A Christian man is a most free lord of all, subject to none. A Christian man is a most dutiful servant of all, subject to all.' 'Subject to none' in respect of his liberty; 'subject to all' in respect of his charity. This, for Paul, is the law of Christ because this was the way of Christ. And in this way, for Paul, the divine purpose underlying Moses' law is vindicated and accomplished."[144]

Love is so important for the ethics of the New Testament. In Galatians we have seen that "the only thing that counts is faith expressing itself through love" (5:6 NIV). We are called to "serve one another humbly in love. For the entire law is fulfilled in keeping this one command: 'Love your neighbor as yourself'" (5:13-14 NIV). We are told that "the fruit of the Spirit is love" (5:22). Love is a fruit of the Spirit, and it is characterized by service and carrying one another's burdens.

In Galatians 5:13 he calls us to serve one another humbly in love. "In love" is a favorite phrase of Paul's: "Let all that you do be done in love" (1 Cor. 16:14), "being rooted and grounded in love" (Eph. 3:17), "with all humility and gentleness with patience, bearing with one another in love" (Eph. 4:2), "speaking the truth in love" (Eph. 4:15), "and walk in love, as the Messiah also loved us and gave himself for us" (Eph. 5:2 CSB), "my goal is that they may be encouraged in heart and united in love" (Col. 2:2 NIV).

---

[144] F.F. Bruce, *Paul: Apostle of the Heart Set Free* (Grand Rapids: Eerdmans, 1977), 201-02.

New Testament scholar Bruce Longenecker writes, "These are qualities that enhance corporate life. Moreover, it may not be coincidental that love appears first in the list, giving it pride of place. Paul has emphasized love on three occasions thus far in his letter, and all of them in important contexts. Not only is love (as opposed to circumcision) the characteristic of those 'in Christ' (5:6; cf. 5:13), it is so precisely because Christians are joined in union with the one who himself demonstrated love (2:20). The love that Christ exhibited is defined further in 2:20 as his self-giving, the same quality that Paul highlights at the start of his letter (1:4). This quality of self-giving love seems, to Paul's mind, to be a wholly eschatological phenomenon, an eschatological quality reproduced in the lives of those united with Christ by means of the Spirit of Christ. It is little wonder, then, that it appears first in the list, since Paul considered it to be the fundamental characteristic of Christ's own life and imagined it to be the context out of which all other Spirit-generated characteristics arise."[145]

Paul wants the "main principle" of Jesus to become the main principle of the church. This is what he is getting at in Galatians 4:19: "My little children, for whom I am again in the anguish of childbirth until Christ is formed in you!" To fulfill the law of Christ is to continually play out in the life of the community the pattern of self-sacrificial love that Jesus revealed in his death.[146] The law of Christ is the law of giving oneself in love and humility to the service of others. To fulfill the law of Christ is to assume the same posture of

---

[145] Bruce Longenecker, *The Triumph of Abraham's God* (Nashville: Abingdon, 1998), 71.

[146] Hays, *Galatians*, 333.

self-sacrificial giving for the sake of others that Jesus demonstrated.[147]

Are you fulfilling the pattern of the Messiah? Is your life characterized by self-sacrifice for the good of your fellow believers? Do you give up your time for the encouragement of others? Do you give of your resources? Are you carrying one another's burdens? This command, like so many others, presupposes you are sharing life together and are aware of the needs of your brothers and sisters. Are you aware of needs around you? Do you open your home to feed and share life with other members? Do you look out for others? Do you pray for one another? Jesus has given his life for us, and we are called to give ourselves for one another. This pattern is vitally important. We have seen it from Philippians 2, and now we see that it is so important that Paul calls it the law of Christ. Next we will see it in Romans 14-15.

---

[147] The pattern of the Messiah is a "way of describing this pattern of renouncing one's own privileges and interests for the sake of others," according to Richard Hays, in "Crucified with Christ: A Synthesis of the Theology of 1 & 2 Thessalonians, Philemon, Philippians, and Galatians," in *Pauline Theology* Vol. 1, ed. Jouette M. Bassler (Minneapolis: Fortress, 1994), 241.

Chapter 11:

Cruciform Love: Even as Christ (Romans 14:1-15:7)

We have seen that biblical love is not abstract but is action grounded in an event. God has loved us, and we are called to imitate his loving action. We need to be robustly cross-centered, finding in the cross *both* the provision for salvation and the pattern of salvation.

The theme of cruciform love is laced throughout the New Testament. This pattern of cruciform love is the foundation upon which all the specific commandments of the Christian life are based.[148] In Romans 14:1-15:7, Paul applies his master story to the issue of secondary matters and unity:

> As for the one who is weak in faith, welcome him, but not to quarrel over opinions. One person believes he may eat anything, while the weak person eats only vegetables. Let not the one who eats despise the one who abstains, and let not the one who abstains pass judgment on the one who eats, for God has welcomed him. Who are you to pass judgment on the servant of another? It is before his own master that he stands or falls. And he will be upheld, for the Lord is able to make him stand. One person esteems one day as better than another, while another esteems all days alike. Each one should be fully convinced in his own mind. The one who observes the day, observes it in honor of the Lord. The one who eats, eats in honor of the Lord, since he gives thanks to God, while the one who abstains, abstains in honor of the Lord and gives thanks to God. For none of us lives to himself, and none of us dies to himself. For if we live, we live to the

---

148 Gorman, *Cruciformity*, 171.

Lord, and if we die, we die to the Lord. So then, whether we live or whether we die, we are the Lord's. For to this end Christ died and lived again, that he might be Lord both of the dead and of the living. Why do you pass judgment on your brother? Or you, why do you despise your brother? For we will all stand before the judgment seat of God; for it is written, "As I live, says the Lord, every knee shall bow to me, and every tongue shall confess to God." So then each of us will give an account of himself to God. Therefore let us not pass judgment on one another any longer, but rather decide never to put a stumbling block or hindrance in the way of a brother. I know and am persuaded in the Lord Jesus that nothing is unclean in itself, but it is unclean for anyone who thinks it unclean. For if your brother is grieved by what you eat, you are no longer walking in love. By what you eat, do not destroy the one for whom Christ died. So do not let what you regard as good be spoken of as evil. For the kingdom of God is not a matter of eating and drinking but of righteousness and peace and joy in the Holy Spirit. Whoever thus serves Christ is acceptable to God and approved by men. So then let us pursue what makes for peace and for mutual upbuilding. Do not, for the sake of food, destroy the work of God. Everything is indeed clean, but it is wrong for anyone to make another stumble by what he eats. It is good not to eat meat or drink wine or do anything that causes your brother to stumble. The faith that you have, keep between yourself and God. Blessed is the one who has no reason to pass judgment on himself for what he approves. But whoever has doubts is condemned if he eats, because the eating is not from faith. For whatever does not proceed from faith is sin. We who are strong have an obligation to bear with the failings of the weak, and not to please ourselves. Let each of us please his neighbor for his good, to build him up. For Christ did not please himself, but as it is written, "The reproaches of those who reproached you fell on me." For whatever was written in former days was written for our instruction, that through endurance and through the encouragement of the Scriptures we might have hope. May the God of endurance and encouragement grant you to live in such harmony with one another, in accord with Christ Jesus, that together you may with one voice glorify the God and Father of our Lord Jesus Christ.

Therefore welcome one another as Christ has welcomed you, for the glory of God.

The Situation

More disunity? Imagine that. It seems like almost every New Testament letter deals with disunity of some sort within the churches. Why is this? Was it because they were more sinful than we are? No, human nature hasn't changed. There will be strife within the community when we are truly living life together. As one has said, "To dwell in love with saints above, oh that will be glory, but to dwell below with saints we know, well that's another story."

Paul is writing to a mixed audience of Jews and Gentiles and has been unpacking the gospel. He has been laboring to explain the significance of the newness that Jesus brings. The new covenant has come, and it has replaced the old covenant. Now, the old way no longer holds. The people of God are no longer defined around the Torah. Salvation is available to Jews and Gentiles. Apparently, there was conflict because the Gentiles (the strong) were not following the law. Paul takes sides with the Gentiles theologically, but he is primarily exhorting the Gentiles as well. In this wonderful passage, Paul gives us three ways to deal with disunity over nonessentials:

Who are You to Judge?

The Holy Spirit moves Paul to write, "Who are you to pass judgment on the servant of another? (14:4).... Why do you pass judgment on your brother? Or you, why do you despise your brother? For we will all stand before the judgment seat of God; for it is written, 'As I live, says the Lord, every knee shall bow to me, and every tongue shall confess to God.' So then each of us will give an account of himself to God. Therefore let us not pass judgment on one another any longer, but rather decide never to put a stumbling block or hindrance in the way of a brother" (14:10-13). So much of the Christian life falls into place when we have a proper view of self and a proper view of God. God alone is the judge. We are mere servants.

Notice that Paul quotes Isaiah 45 here. What is fascinating is that, as shown above in Philippians 2:10, Paul quotes the exact same passage but applies it to Jesus! In context, it is *YHWH* who all will bow to. Paul can use the same passage to refer to God the Son and God the Father, proving that Jesus is fully God and fully man.

Paul is insisting that we should just look out for ourselves when it comes to disputable matters. As a side note, I want to make an observation about the Sabbath that is mentioned in this passage. Paul says each should be fully convinced in his own mind (14:5). This is a far cry from "Thou shall keep the Sabbath day holy or die." Do you remember the guy who was stoned for gathering wood on the Sabbath? Times have changed. The important point Paul makes, though, is do not judge each other over the issue.

Know What Time it is

Jesus brought about the new covenant, which replaced the old covenant. In the old covenant, the law was all about externals: what to eat, what not to eat; what to wear, what not to wear; what days to work, what day not to work. All that has changed now. We are no longer bound to the law but are bound to Jesus. He has already made this clear in Romans; in 6:14, he said that we are no longer under law but under grace. In Romans 7:4-6, he said, "Likewise, my brothers, you also have died to the law through the body of Christ, so that you may belong to another, to him who has been raised from the dead, in order that we may bear fruit for God. For while we were living in the flesh, our sinful passions, aroused by the law, were at work in our members to bear fruit for death. But now we are released from the law, having died to that which held us captive, so that we serve in the new way of the Spirit and not in the old way of the written code."

In this passage, he shows that the old ways have passed. He wrote, "I know and am persuaded in the Lord Jesus that nothing is unclean in itself (14).... For the kingdom of God is not a matter of eating and drinking but of righteousness and peace and joy in the Holy Spirit (17).... Everything is indeed clean" (20).

It is important to note that according to this passage, it is wrong to violate conscience, but our conscience can be informed. Paul's was a very zealous Jew, but Jesus and his new ways informed and corrected his conscience:

> And he called the people to him again and said to them, "Hear me, all of you, and understand: There is nothing outside a person that by going into him can defile him, but the things that come out of a person are what defile him." And when he had entered the house and left the people, his disciples asked him about the parable. And he said to them, "Then are you also without understanding? Do you not see that whatever goes into a person from outside cannot defile him, since it enters not his heart but his stomach, and is expelled?" (Thus he declared all foods clean.) And he said, "What comes out of a person is what defiles him. For from within, out of the heart of man, come evil thoughts, sexual immorality, theft, murder, adultery, coveting, wickedness, deceit, sensuality, envy, slander, pride, foolishness. (Mark 7:14-22)

Put Others Before Yourselves

Now we come to the important section for the purpose of this book. Paul writes, "We who are strong have an obligation to bear with the failings of the weak, and not to please ourselves. Let each of us please his neighbor for his good, to build him up. For Christ did not please himself, but as it is written, 'The reproaches of those who reproached you fell on me'" (Rom. 15:1-3). The phrase "we who are strong ought to bear" could be translated as "we who are strong have a debt to bear" (*opheilomen*). This alludes back to Romans 13:8 where he wrote "Owe [*opheilete*] no one anything, except to love each other, for the one who loves another has fulfilled the law."

The verb "bear" (*bastazo*) alludes to Matthew 8:17, where Matthew quotes Isaiah to say Jesus "bore" our diseases. It is also the same verb Paul uses in Galatians 6:2 when he says we should "bear" one another's burdens and in this way we will fill out the pattern of self-enslaving love modeled by our Savior. The Revised English Bible translates Romans 15:3 this way: "Those of us who are strong must accept as our own burden the tender scruples of the weak."

We will be helped to put the weak before ourselves by realizing that we too are weak. Several chapters earlier, Paul wrote, "For while we were still weak, Christ died for the ungodly" (Rom. 5:6).

We should put others first because this is exactly what Jesus taught. The word "neighbor" echoes back to the great commandment. This word is used 16 times in the New Testament and all but three of them are found in quotations of or allusions to the love command of Leviticus 19:18: "You shall love your neighbor as yourself."[149] In John 13:34, Jesus told his disciples, "A new commandment I give to you, that you love one another: just as I have loved you, you also are

---

[149] Douglas J. Moo, *The Epistle to the Romans* (Grand Rapids: Eerdmans, 1996), 867.

to love one another." Back to the passage in Romans we are focusing on. The centrality of love is taught throughout:

Romans 12:9— *"Let love be genuine."*

Romans 12:10— *"Love one another with brotherly affection."*

Romans 13:8-10— *"Owe no one anything, except to love each other, for the one who loves another has fulfilled the law. For the commandments, "You shall not commit adultery, You shall not murder, You shall not steal, You shall not covet," and any other commandment, are summed up in this word: "You shall love your neighbor as yourself." Love does no wrong to a neighbor; therefore love is the fulfilling of the law."*

Romans 14:15— *"For if your brother is grieved by what you eat, you are no longer walking in love."*

Romans 14:19— *"So then let us pursue what makes for peace and for mutual upbuilding."*

Love was important for Paul because love was important for Jesus. We should put others before ourselves because that's what Jesus *did*. Notice how Paul grounds his exhortation not to please ourselves but please our neighbors for their edification: for even Christ did not please himself![150] As Richard Hays notes, "Jesus was willing to die for these people, says Paul, and you aren't even willing to modify

---

[150] James Dunn writes, "To fulfill the law of Christ is to bear one another's burdens, which is a particular example of loving the neighbor, which fulfills the law. The point should be obvious: in the parallel trains of thought, 'the law of Christ' (Galatians) is equivalent to Jesus' refusal to please himself (Romans). Which presumably means that in Paul's mind 'the law of Christ' includes some reference to Jesus' own example," in "'The Law of Faith,' 'the Law of the Spirit' and 'the Law of Christ'" in *Theology and Ethics*, edited by Eugene H. Lovering, Jr. and Jerry L. Sumney (Nashville: Abingdon, 1996), 76.

your diet?"[151] Paul doesn't give them a list of rules but points them to a person.

Paul appeals to Psalm 69, which represents the attitude and prayer of Jesus at his death. He took on suffering for the sake of others. Paul quotes it to appeal to Jesus' giving of himself in service to others as a model to imitate.[152]

Notice the similarities between Romans 15:1-3, Philippians 2, and Galatians 5:

> Romans 15:1-3—*Bear the burdens of the weak, don't please yourself but please your neighbor for their good because Christ did not please himself but gave of self for our good (bore the insults we deserved).*

> Philippians 2:3-8—*Do nothing out of selfishness. Rather, in humility value others above yourselves, not looking to your own interests but to the interests of others. Have the same mindset of Jesus who gave of himself for our good.*

> Galatians 5:13—*Although you are free, don't use your freedom to indulge the flesh. Rather become slaves of one another humbly in love.*

Cruciform love is the primary Christian virtue!

Finally, we should put others first so that we will be united and give God glory. Romans 15:5-7 reads: "May the God of endurance and encouragement grant you to live in such harmony with one another, in accord with Christ Jesus, that together you may with one voice glorify the God and Father of our Lord Jesus Christ. Therefore welcome one another as Christ has welcomed you, for the glory of God."

Notice again the parallels to what Michael Gorman calls "Paul's Master Story" (Philippians 2:3-10):

---

[151] Hays, *The Moral Vision of the New Testament*, 28.

[152] Moo, *Romans*, 869.

Philippians 2:2—*"Complete my joy by being of the same mind (auto phronete), having the same love, being in full accord and of one mind."*

Romans 15:5-6—*"May the God of endurance and encouragement grant you to live in such harmony (auto phronein) with one another, in accord with Christ Jesus, that together you may with one voice glorify the God and Father of our Lord Jesus Christ."*

Philippians 2:5—*"In your relationships with one another, have the same mindset as Christ Jesus" (NIV).*

Michael Gorman writes, "In Romans 15, Christ's dying is a paradigmatic act of burden-bearing and others-pleasing love that can engender a host of analogous acts by Paul and his communities."[153] Just think about how our relationships would be transformed if we adopted the Jesus mindset. Sibling to sibling relationships would change. Marriages would begin to reflect Christ and the church. Co-workers would ask why you give of self for their good. Don't please yourself, but give of yourself for the building up of your neighbor, for this is what your Lord did![154]

---

[153] Gorman, *Cruciformity,* 172.

[154] J.R. Daniel Kirk writes, "The love a Christian community is none other than the continuing embodiment of the self-giving love of Jesus. The ethic of Jesus is comprised of a self-giving life of love, the giving up of self so that the other might live," in *Jesus I have Loved, but Paul?* (Grand Rapids: Baker Academic, 2011), 79.

Chapter 12:

Cruciform Love: Its Centrality
(1 Corinthians 13)

Do you have a junk drawer? You know, the place where anything and everything goes? The drawer that is not really set aside for anything in particular? Love is a "junk drawer" term. We use it for all sorts of things. I love Tex-Mex, and I love my son. I love basketball, and I love my wife. Hopefully these are different types of "love." Usually when we say we love something, we do so for what it can do for me. I love what I appreciate in this moment. Obviously love is wearing too many hats. As T.J. Deidun notes, "The term 'love' is notoriously ambiguous; it can mean everything and nothing; it can capture the essence of Christianity [sic] and it can sum up a 'philosophy' that is basically non-religious and, in the last analysis, anti-Christian."[155] As text after text has demonstrated, biblical love has a specific meaning.

God has loved us in Christ's cross, and we are called to imitate his loving action. To act lovingly, to have love means to be toward others the way God in Christ has been toward us.[156] As Leon Morris puts it, "The Christians thought of love as that quality we see on the cross. It is a love for the utterly unworthy, a love that proceeds from a God who is love. It is a love lavished on others without a

---

[155] T.J. Deidun, *New Covenant Morality in Paul* (Rome: Biblical Institute, 1981), 234.

[156] Gordon Fee, *The First Epistle to the Corinthians,* NICNT (Grand Rapids: Eerdmans, 1987), 631.

thought whether they are worthy or not. It proceeds from the nature of the lover, not from any attractiveness in the beloved. The Christian who has experienced God's love for him while he was yet a sinner (Rom. 5:8) has been transformed by the experience. Now he sees people as those for whom Christ died, the objects of God's love, and therefore the objects of the love of God's people. In his measure, he comes to practice the love that seeks nothing for itself, but only the good of the loved one. It is this love that the apostle unfolds."[157]

Many of us are familiar with 1 Corinthians 13 from marriage sermons, but this chapter is not referring to marriage (although I do think it is okay to apply it to marriage). First Corinthians 13 is the M.O. (the mode of operation) for the use of spiritual gifts.[158] One scholar has written that this is "the greatest, strongest, deepest thing Paul ever wrote."[159] Here Paul shows us what true spirituality is:

> If I speak in the tongues of men and of angels, but have not love, I am a noisy gong or a clanging cymbal. And if I have prophetic powers, and understand all mysteries and all knowledge, and if I have all faith, so as to remove mountains, but have not love, I am nothing. If I give away all I have, and if I deliver up my body to be burned, but have not love, I gain nothing. Love is patient and kind; love does not envy or boast; it is not arrogant or rude. It does not insist on its own way; it is not irritable or resentful; it does not rejoice at wrongdoing, but rejoices with the truth. Love bears all things, believes all things, hopes all things, endures all things. Love never ends. As for prophecies, they will pass away; as for tongues, they will cease; as for

---

[157] Leon Morris, *1 Corinthians*, TNTC (Grand Rapids: Eerdmans, 1985), 177.

[158] Gorman, *Cruciformity*, 236.

[159] Adolf Harnack, quoted in Morris, *1 Corinthians*, 176.

knowledge, it will pass away. For we know in part and we prophesy in part, but when the perfect comes, the partial will pass away. When I was a child, I spoke like a child, I thought like a child, I reasoned like a child. When I became a man, I gave up childish ways. For now we see in a mirror dimly, but then face to face. Now I know in part; then I shall know fully, even as I have been fully known. So now faith, hope, and love abide, these three; but the greatest of these is love. (1 Cor. 13:1-13).

This chapter breaks down quite nicely: the necessity of love (1-3), the character of love (4-7), and the endurance of love (8-13).

The Necessity of Love (1-3)

Love is absolutely necessary. It doesn't matter what you can do; if it is not done in love, it is worthless. Paul describes loveless service as an annoying noise, a resounding gong, and a clanging cymbal. In other words, if you lack love, you just give people headaches. Prophecy is a catchall term for any type of intelligible speech uttered by members of the congregation for the edification of another.[160] Knowledge is referring to knowledge of God's ways in the present age. "Mystery" is normally a revelation term in Paul and could refer to knowledge of the Scriptures. Without love, these things are worthless. If we lack love, we are nothing *in the sight of God*.[161]

Should I say it again? Love is absolutely necessary! Colossians 3:14 says, "And above all these put on love, which binds everything together in perfect harmony." In John 13, Jesus said that all people will know that we are his disciples by our love for one another. As Jon Zens writes, "The one

---

[160] John Dickson, *The Best Kept Secret of Christian Mission* (Grand Rapids: Zondervan, 2010), 168.

[161] Fee, *The First Epistle to the Corinthians*, 632.

characteristic that he isolates as bearing testimony to the world about the reality of the Christian faith is brotherly love. Not right doctrine, nor denominational creeds, nor persuasive preaching, nor impressive sanctuaries, nor elaborate social programs, nor vast numbers, but genuine and discernible love between believers."[162]

From verse 3, we also see that love is not *merely* action. There is a type of service that is futile. This gets to the heart level. Outward obedience is fairly easy, but true obedience is from the heart. Biblically defined, love is primarily action, but our hearts should follow. Paul gives an example of a person who gives all their possessions away to the poor and even physically suffers, *but does not have love.* Biblically speaking, love is primarily action, but that's not the end of the story. As C.S. Lewis writes, "The rule for all of us is perfectly simple. Do not waste time bothering whether you 'love' your neighbor; act as if you did. As soon as we do this, we find one of the great secrets. When you are behaving as if you loved someone, you will presently come to love him.... [love] is quite distinct from affection, yet it leads to affection."[163]

So what do you deem to be spiritually significant? Bible reading? Preaching? Evangelizing? Discipling your children? All these are important, but if you do these things without love, you gain nothing!

The Character of Love (4-7)

Paul starts with a passive and active aspect of love. It is patient; it "suffereth long" (KJV). This is the passive aspect.

---

[162] Jon Zens, "This is My Beloved Son, Hear Him," *Searching Together* 25.1-3 (Summer-Winter 1997), 13.

[163] C.S. Lewis, *Mere Christianity*, 110.

The active aspect is kindness. Kindness is active goodness on the behalf of others.[164] Love does not envy. There is to be no rivalry or competition within the people of God. It does not boast. It does not act in a self-centered manner in order to call attention to oneself. It is impossible to boast and love at the same time. Boasting is self-oriented and love is others-oriented. The two are mutually exclusive. You cannot seek to build up self while seeking to build up others. Love is not proud. It is not puffed up. It is not rude. It does not dishonor others.

I want to press in on a phrase in verse five. Love isn't selfish; it does not insist on its own way. This is the negative aspect of cruciform love. The opposite of not insisting on one's own way is insisting on the way of others. Cruciform love has a negative and positive aspect. It is two-dimensional. It does not seek its own advantage (negative), but seeks the good of others (positive). It is not self-oriented but other-oriented. Cruciform love is giving of self for the good of others.[165] Love builds up. Paul has already been pounding this home to the Corinthians:

8:1 — *"Now concerning food offered to idols: we know that 'all of us possess knowledge.' This 'knowledge' puffs up, but love builds up."*

10:24 — *"Let no one seek his own good, but the good of his neighbor."*

10:32-11:1 — *"Give no offense to Jews or to Greeks or to the church of God, just as I try to please everyone in everything I do, not seeking my own advantage, but that of many, that they may be saved. Be imitators of me, as I am of Christ."*

---

[164] Fee, *The First Epistle to the Corinthians*, 636.

[165] Gorman, *Cruciformity*, 160.

14:1-5—*"Pursue love, and earnestly desire the spiritual gifts, especially that you may prophesy. For one who speaks in a tongue speaks not to men but to God; for no one understands him, but he utters mysteries in the Spirit. On the other hand, the one who prophesies speaks to people for their upbuilding and encouragement and consolation. The one who speaks in a tongue builds up himself, but the one who prophesies builds up the church. Now I want you all to speak in tongues, but even more to prophesy. The one who prophesies is greater than the one who speaks in tongues, unless someone interprets, so that the church may be built up."*

14:12—*"So with yourselves, since you are eager for manifestations of the Spirit, strive to excel in building up the church."*

14:26—*"What then, brothers? When you come together, each one has a hymn, a lesson, a revelation, a tongue, or an interpretation. Let all things be done for building up."*

If cruciform love is giving of self for the good of others, what is their ultimate good? Salvation! In 1 Corinthians 9:19-23, Paul applies cruciform love to mission:

For though I am free from all, I have made myself a servant to all, that I might win more of them. To the Jews I became as a Jew, in order to win Jews. To those under the law I became as one under the law (though not being myself under the law) that I might win those under the law. To those outside the law I became as one outside the law (not being outside the law of God but under the law of Christ) that I might win those outside the law. To the weak I became weak, that I might win the weak. I have become all things to all people, that by all means I might save some. I do it all for the sake of the gospel, that I may share with them in its blessings.

Paul seeks to serve his audience for their good (for their salvation). He gives of himself (makes himself a slave) so that many will be saved. When Paul says that he is under Christ's law, he does not mean that he is under a new legal code, but now Christ is his new norm. We are to be obedient to him.[166] As Richard Hays writes, "By using the expression 'under Christ's law' (cf. Gal. 6:2), Paul does not mean that he has acquired a new legal code of commandments to obey (such as the teachings of Jesus); rather, he is asserting that the pattern of Christ's self-sacrificial death on a cross has now become the normative pattern for his own existence."[167]

Continuing our examination of the character of love we see that love keeps no record of wrong. There is no room for grudges in the Christian life. Let go of past offenses—for their sake and yours. Love doesn't delight in evil but rejoices with the truth. I am afraid that too many Christians do the opposite of this. They delight in evil and are ashamed of the truth. Love always hopes and trusts. Love is optimistic; it is eager to believe the best.

These things are, of course, rooted in God's character. God is patient. He holds back his wrath towards us. God is kind. Christian, consider the thousandfold expressions of his mercy—even today. He is not easily angered. He keeps no record of wrongs. Second Corinthians 5:19 says, "In Christ God was reconciling the world to himself, not counting their trespasses against them." Psalm 103:11-12 reads, "For as high as the heavens are above the earth, so great is his steadfast love toward those who fear him; as far as the east is from the west, so far does he remove our transgressions from us." The east is a long way from the west. Jeremiah 31:34 reads, "For I will forgive their iniquity, and I will remember their sin no more." God doesn't delight in evil; he

---

[166] Hans Conzelmann, *1 Corinthians* (Philadelphia: Fortress Press, 1975), 161. See also Ben Witherington, *Conflict and Community in Corinth* (Grand Rapids: Eerdmans, 1995), 213.

[167] Hays, *First Corinthians*, 154.

rejoices with the truth. We see that the character of love is rooted in the character of God.

Love's Endurance (8-13)

Why should you worry with cruciform love? Because it is permanent! Love is not a duty; it is our destiny.[168] Don't focus too much on tongues and prophecy, writes Paul, for they are temporary. Love, however, is eternal. "Completeness" in verse ten refers to the end of the age, the eschaton. First Corinthians 1:7 says, "Therefore you do not lack any spiritual gift as you eagerly wait for our Lord Jesus Christ to be revealed" (NIV). Then the gifts that are now necessary to build up the church will no longer be needed. When the sun rises, the candle can be blown out. Childhood means the present age while manhood represents the eternal state. The gifts are for childhood, the present age.

In verse 13, Paul mentions his famous triad: faith, hope, and love. By focusing on love, we are learning the language of the new creation. It *abides*. Love is a bridge from this world to the next. As Karl Barth wrote, "It is love alone that counts; it is love alone that triumphs; it is love alone that endures."[169]

Have you grasped the love of Christ for you so that you now pour out love for others? Can you substitute your name for the noun *love* in this chapter? Lord, make it so. I want to conclude by sharing Eugene Peterson's paraphrase of this wonderful chapter:

> If I speak with human eloquence and angelic ecstasy but don't love, I'm nothing but the creaking of a rusty gate. If I

---

[168] Wright, *After You Believe*, 188.

[169] Karl Barth, *Church Dogmatics* IV/2 (Edinburgh: T&T Clark International), 824-40.

speak God's Word with power, revealing all his mysteries and
making everything plain as day, and if I have faith that says to
a mountain, "Jump," and it jumps, but I don't love, I'm nothing. If I give everything I own to the poor and even go to the
stake to be burned as a martyr, but I don't love, I've gotten
nowhere. So, no matter what I say, what I believe, and what I
do, I'm bankrupt without love. Love never gives up. Love
cares more for others than for self. Love doesn't want what it
doesn't have. Love doesn't strut, doesn't have a swelled head,
doesn't force itself on others, isn't always "me first," doesn't fly
off the handle, doesn't keep score of the sins of others, doesn't
revel when others grovel, takes pleasure in the flowering of
truth, puts up with anything, trusts God always, always looks
for the best, never looks back, but keeps going to the end. Love
never dies. Inspired speech will be over some day; praying in
tongues will end; understanding will reach its limit. We know
only a portion of the truth, and what we say about God is always incomplete. But when the Complete arrives, our incom-
pletes will be canceled. When I was an infant at my mother's
breast, I gurgled and cooed like any infant. When I grew up, I
left those infant ways for good. We don't yet see things clearly.
We're squinting in a fog, peering through a mist. But it won't
be long before the weather clears and the sun shines bright!
We'll see it all then, see it all as clearly as God sees us, know-
ing him directly just as he knows us! But for right now, until
that completeness, we have three things to do to lead us toward that consummation: trust steadily in God, hope un-
swervingly, love extravagantly. And the best of the three is
love [The Message].

Chapter 13:

Cruciform Love:
As Christ Loved the Church
(Ephesians 5:22-33)

So far in this book, cruciform love has been seen as essentially a commitment of the will to give of self for the good of another. Cruciform love is "cross-shaped" love. First John 3:16 says, "By this we know love, that he laid down his life for us, and we ought to lay down our lives for the brothers." Love is defined by the cross of Christ. It has been shown that neighbor-love is taught throughout the New Testament. For those of us who are married, our nearest neighbor is obviously our spouse. If you are married, you are a walking, talking sermon. Through your marriage, you are constantly preaching a gospel; the question is whether or not our sermons are biblical.

The book of Ephesians is easily outlined. Chapters 1-3 describe the *creation* of the new humanity while chapters 4-6 describe the *conduct* of the new humanity. So in Ephesians 4:1, we read, " I *therefore*, a prisoner for the Lord, urge you to walk in a manner worthy of the calling to which you have been called" (my italics). Notice the "therefore." Paul is saying, based upon the gospel theology I have laid out, *therefore* live this way. In Ephesians 5:18, the Holy Spirit through Paul commanded the Ephesians to be filled with the Spirit. He then unpacks that command with five activities: speaking, singing, making music, giving thanks, and submitting. Part of being filled with the Spirit then is submitting to divinely ordered relationships.[170] Hear the words of Ephesians 5:22-33:

> *Wives, submit to your own husbands, as to the Lord. For the husband is the head of the wife even as Christ is the head of the church, his body, and is himself its Savior. Now as the church submits to Christ, so also wives should submit in everything to their husbands. Husbands, love your wives, as Christ loved the church and gave himself up for her, that he might sanctify her, having cleansed her by the washing of water with the word, so that he might present the church to himself in splendor, without spot or wrinkle or any such thing, that she might be holy and without blemish. In the same way husbands should love their wives as their own bodies. He who loves his wife loves himself. For no one ever hated his own flesh, but nourishes and cherishes it, just as Christ does the church, because we are members of his body. "Therefore a man shall leave his father and mother and hold fast to his wife, and the two shall become one flesh." This mystery is profound, and I am saying that it refers to Christ and the church. However, let each one of you love his wife as himself, and let the wife see that she respects her husband.*

Paul begins with the wives: "Wives, submit to your own husbands, as to the Lord. For the husband is the head of the wife even as Christ is the head of the church, his body, and is himself its Savior. Now as the church submits to Christ, so also wives should submit in everything to their husbands." He commands the wives to submit to their husbands. Wives are called to submit to their husbands *because* he is the head of the home. The Bible does not teach that women should submit to men but that wives should submit to their husbands.

---

[170] Peter T. O'Brien, *The Letter to the Ephesians* (Grand Rapids: Eerdmans, 1999), 398-99.

God is God. God's Word is God's word. In our current cultural situation, submission is a bad word, but it mustn't be among the people of God. *He* has spoken. *He* has established certain leadership and authority roles within the family, and submission is a humble recognition of that divine ordering.[171] This is not a suggestion. This is *the* Christian view of the home. First Corinthians 11:3 says that "the head of every man is Christ, the head of a wife is her husband, and the head of Christ is God"; First Corinthians 11:7-9 reads, "For a man ought not to cover his head, since he is the image and glory of God, but woman is the glory of man. For man was not made from woman, but woman from man. Neither was man created for woman, but woman for man"; First Peter 3:1 reads, "Likewise, wives, be subject to your own husbands"; First Peter 3:5-6: "For this is how the holy women who hoped in God used to adorn themselves, by submitting to their own husbands, as Sarah obeyed Abraham, calling him lord. And you are her children, if you do good and do not fear anything that is frightening"; Colossians 3:18 reads, "Wives, submit to your husbands, as is fitting in the Lord"; Titus 2:5 says women should learn "to love their husbands and children, to be self-controlled, pure, working at home, kind, and submissive to their own husbands, that the word of God may not be reviled." The New Testament has one voice on the issue of gender roles.

John Piper defines submission as "the divine calling of a wife to honor and affirm her husband's leadership and help

---

171 Ibid., 411.

carry it through according to her gifts."[172] He goes on to say what submission is not:

- It does not mean agreeing with everything your husband says.
- It does not mean leaving your will or your brain at the wedding altar.
- It does not mean avoiding every effort to change a husband.
- It does not mean putting the will of the husband before the will of Christ.
- It does not mean that a wife gets her personal, spiritual strength primarily through her husband.
- It does not mean that a wife is to act out of fear.[173]

Submission does not imply that the wife is inferior in dignity than the husband. The analogy of the Trinity is helpful here. The persons of the Trinity are equal in authority but have differing roles. The Son is fully God, but submits to the Father. The Son always does the things that are pleasing to the Father (John 8:28-29). The Son does nothing on his own authority. The Son's food is to do the Father's will.[174]

Wives are called to submit to their husbands *as the church submits to Christ.* How does the church submit to Christ? By looking to Christ her head for beneficial rule, living by his norms, experiencing his loving presence, receiving from

---

[172] John Piper, *This Momentary Marriage* (Wheaton, IL: Crossway, 2009), 80.

[173] Ibid., 99-101.

[174] See Bruce Ware's helpful book, *Father, Son, and Holy Spirit* (Wheaton: Crossway, 2005).

him gifts that will enable growth, and responding to him in gratitude and awe.[175]

Wives are called to submit to their husbands *as to the Lord*. Wife, your discipleship is now bound up with your husband. To submit to him is to submit to the Lord. Wives are to submit to their husbands *in everything*. Submission must occur in every area of life. This means that now there is no area of your life where you say to your husband, "Back off, this is mine."

Verse 33 says, "However, let each one of you love his wife as himself, and let the wife see that she respects her husband." The wife is called to submit to and respect her husband. Wife, does your husband feel respected by you? This is one of his most important needs. I hope you are deeply familiar with the "Proverbs 31 woman." Have you ever noticed that it says that her husband is respected at the city gate? All too often husbands are pitied at the city gate because their wife complains and talks behind his back rather than praises him there. Wives, do not complain about your husband; respect him.

Husbands, you are the head of the home. Again, verse 23 says, "For the husband is the head of the wife even as Christ is the head of the church, his body, and is himself its Savior." Piper defines headship as "the divine calling of a husband to take primary responsibility for Christlike, servant leadership, protection, and provision in the home."[176] This is how God ordered things. Genesis 3 says that *Eve* took the fruit, ate it, and gave it to Adam but God comes and says *to the man*, "Where are you" (Gen. 3:9)? The husband is the

---

[175] O'Brien, *Ephesians*, 416.

[176] Piper, *This Momentary Marriage*, 80.

head. He is the responsible leader. Husband, you are called to lead your home.

Husband, as head of the home you are called to be the spiritual leader. This is your God-given responsibility. Are you leading your wife in prayer? Are you leading her in reading and understanding God's Word? In First Corinthians 14, Paul says that women should remain silent in the churches and that if they have questions, they should ask their husbands at home (1 Cor. 14:35). Are you prepared to answer those questions? Do you lead in reading God-centered books? Start simple. You don't have to know Greek and Hebrew to lead your wife in learning and following God's Word. I challenge you: today after dinner read a chapter of the Bible and pray with your wife before you go to bed. It is a very easy way to start. She will love you for it.

Husband, are you the chief repenter? You are obviously not called to be sinless. You will fail, but when you fail, you are called to lead in confession and repentance. Let me share my latest "mess-up" as an illustration. Recently the elders of our church went to a men's conference to learn about biblical masculinity. We were getting settled in our seats, ready to be wrecked afresh by the Holy Spirit. As I was sitting, I felt my phone vibrate in my pocket. It was a number I did not recognize, and the service was about to start, so I ignored it, or at least attempted to. The same number called again. I decided I had better answer it in case something was wrong. Sure enough, it was my wife. She had accidentally locked her keys in her trunk. I was thirty minutes away. Her cell phone was locked in the car so I gave her some numbers of our church members so she could get a ride home. She called some ladies and called me back. Now, we had talked about this before. We had a rule: never, ever put the keys in the trunk because if you never put the keys in the trunk you will never have to worry about locking them in there. At this point, my idiot self thought it would be helpful to remind her of our rule: if she had never put the keys in the trunk, this would not have happened. She gently responded, "I understand that, Blake." I wish I could have seen her heart at that moment. I imagine she was giving me a roundhouse karate kick to the throat. As soon as the words left my mouth, I knew I was in the wrong. We got off the phone, and then I called her right back to repent. I confessed that that was a stupid, unhelpful, and needless comment.

Why do I share that story? I do so to show that I am a "work in progress," but also to make the point that what is important is confession and repentance. I should have never made that comment. I also should have never got off the phone. I should've repented on the spot. Fights will happen. Conflict is inevitable. What is important is constant and continual confession and repentance. Husband, you should be the first to confess and repent of your sin.

Paul Tripp writes, "Enough of pointing the finger. Enough of listening to your inner lawyer defend your cause. Enough of carrying around a record of your spouse's wrongs. Enough of judging, criticizing, and blaming. Enough of holding the other to a higher standard than the one you hold for yourself. Enough of complaining, arguing, withdrawing, and manipulating. Enough of the self-righteous standoff that never leads to change. Enough of hurt and acrimony. Enough of painting yourself as the victim and your spouse as the criminal. Enough of demanding and entitlement. Enough of threat and guilt. Enough of telling the other how good you are and how thankful she should be to live with a person like you. Enough of going to bed in angry, self-righteous silence. Enough of hyper-vigilantly watching him to see if he is delivering. Enough of looking to him to be your personal messiah, satisfying the longings of your heart. Enough. It is time to quit pointing the finger and to start confessing how deep and pervasive your weakness is. Change in your marriage begins with confessing your need."[177]

If you are single, if you want to be married, what are you doing now to prepare to be a husband? We spend 12-16 years preparing for our profession or occupation but often just jump blindly into our more fundamental calling: husband and father. Redeem the time: read good marriage books, be mentored, ask questions of those who are a few steps ahead of you.

Randy Stinson provides 9 areas for you to lead with intention:

- Vision: this is where we are going
- Direction: this is how we get there
- Instruction: let me show you how
- Imitation: watch me
- Inspiration: isn't this great
- Affirmation: you're doing great
- Evaluation: how are we doing
- Correction: let's make a change
- Protection: I'll take care of you[178]

Okay, enough sermonizing. What does this passage have to do with cruciform love? Verse 25 says, "Husbands, love

---

[177] Paul David Tripp, *What Did You Expect?* (Wheaton: Crossway, 2010), 122-23.

[178] Randy Stinson and Dan Dumas, *A Guide to Biblical Manhood* (Louisville: The Southern Baptist Theological Seminary, 2011), 80-83.

your wives, as Christ loved the church and gave himself up for her." We are called to love like Christ. We are called to servant-leadership. "Woman, give me the remote" is a far cry from servant leadership. This love is not simply an emotion but an act of the will. The character and description of love is the phrase "and gave himself up for her."[179] Ephesians 5:1-2 similarly says, "Therefore be imitators of God, as beloved children. And walk in love, as Christ loved us and gave himself up for us, a fragrant offering and sacrifice to God." Paul Tripp defines love as "willing self-sacrifice for the good of another that does not require reciprocation or that the person being loved is deserving."[180]

How did Christ exercise his authority? He took the initiative. He loved with self-giving sacrifice for the church. He washed feet! This love gives of self. This is pouring yourself out for your wife's good. This is working late to come home to work. This is bending over backward to serve her. Her good should be on your mind at all times. C.S. Lewis writes, "This verse [5:25] is most embodied in the husband whose wife receives most and gives the least; it's the one whose wife is most unworthy of him, is—in her own mere nature—least lovable. For the church has no beauty but what the bridegroom gives her; he does not find, but makes her lovely."[181]

First Peter 3:7 reads, "Likewise, husbands, live with your wives in an understanding way, showing honor to the woman as the weaker vessel, since they are heirs with you of the grace of life, so that your prayers may not be hin-

---

[179] O'Brien, *Ephesians*, 419.

[180] Tripp, *What Did You Expect?*, 188.

[181] C.S. Lewis, *The Four Loves* (Harcourt Brace, 1991), 105-06.

dered." Colossians 3:19 says, "Husbands, love your wives, and do not be harsh with them."

Christ intercedes for his church. Do you pray for your wife regularly? I think you should do it every day. Also, any time she has a concern, stop then and there and pray with her and for her. Husband, study your wife. Do you know what blesses her? Where does she need encouragement? What's weighing on her heart today? Do you romance her? You should. Date her. Take initiative. Plan. Surprise her. Focus on connection. Work through challenges. Save and spend on big getaways occasionally. Cultivate your marriage!

Verses 28-31 say, "In the same way husbands should love their wives as their own bodies. He who loves his wife loves himself. For no one ever hated his own flesh, but nourishes and cherishes it, just as Christ does the church, because we are members of his body. 'Therefore a man shall leave his father and mother and hold fast to his wife, and the two shall become one flesh.'" Husbands are called to love their wives like they love themselves. Paul is not saying we first need to have self-love to love our wife, but he is referring to the fact that all people look after their own interests and welfare instinctively. We are now one flesh, one entity. You don't need anyone to tell you to get a drink when you are thirsty or grab a bite when hungry. You take care of yourself instinctively, and you need to take care of your wife instinctively as well.

A key problem for many marriages is laziness. We want to just sit back, put it in cruise, and hopefully things will get better or at least maintain, but not in this world. Satan is on a crusade to wreck marriages. He hates marriage because it points to Christ and his bride. We must wake up and pay attention. Don't drift. Don't be rocked to sleep by the regularity. Don't be numbed by the normalness of it. Can you say that your relationship is the best it has ever been and that it is getting better all the time? Are you growing deeper in unity, love, and understanding? Do you have deeper affection, a more intimate friendship, greater admiration and appreciation, and more tenderness toward your spouse than you did five years ago? These things are not a way of life you wander into. They are blessings from living together with cruciform love. As Paul Tripp writes, "A healthy marriage is a healthy marriage because, by God's grace, the people in that marriage never stop working on it!"[182] We must be committed to doing the moment by moment, day by day things that keep our marriages healthy.

What's the point of such love? Verses 26-27 say that Christ loved the church by giving himself for her "that he might sanctify her, having cleansed her by the washing of water with the word, so that he might present the church to himself in splendor, without spot or wrinkle or any such thing, that she might be holy and without blemish." With these words, Paul is probably referring to the picture painted in Ezekiel 16. There we have a beautiful picture painted for us:

> *Again the word of the LORD came to me: "Son of man, make known to Jerusalem her abominations, and say, Thus says the Lord GOD to Jerusalem: Your origin and your birth are of the land of the Canaanites; your father was an Amorite and your mother a Hittite. And as for your birth, on the day you were born your cord was not cut, nor were you washed with water to cleanse you, nor rubbed with salt, nor wrapped in swaddling cloths. No eye pitied you, to do any of these things to you out of compassion for you, but you were cast*

---

[182] Tripp, *What Did You Expect?* 108.

out on the open field, for you were abhorred, on the day that you were born. And when I passed by you and saw you wallowing in your blood, I said to you in your blood, 'Live!' I said to you in your blood, 'Live!' I made you flourish like a plant of the field. And you grew up and became tall and arrived at full adornment. Your breasts were formed, and your hair had grown; yet you were naked and bare. When I passed by you again and saw you, behold, you were at the age for love, and I spread the corner of my garment over you and covered your nakedness; I made my vow to you and entered into a covenant with you, declares the Lord GOD, and you became mine. Then I bathed you with water and washed off your blood from you and anointed you with oil. I clothed you also with embroidered cloth and shod you with fine leather. I wrapped you in fine linen and covered you with silk. And I adorned you with ornaments and put bracelets on your wrists and a chain on your neck. And I put a ring on your nose and earrings in your ears and a beautiful crown on your head. Thus you were adorned with gold and silver, and your clothing was of fine linen and silk and embroidered cloth. You ate fine flour and honey and oil. You grew exceedingly beautiful and advanced to royalty. And your renown went forth among the nations because of your beauty, for it was perfect through the splendor that I had bestowed on you, declares the Lord GOD. (Ezek. 16:1-14)

Husbands, our calling is to love our wives like Christ loved the church. Are we an agent of sanctification in her life? Are we cleansing her with the word? Are we influencing her towards Christ-likeness?

Verse 32 gives us the divine intention behind the institution of marriage: "This mystery is profound, and I am saying that it refers to Christ and the church." Married couple, what kind of sermon are you preaching? Do people look at your marriage and see resemblances of Christ and his church? Wife, do people see you submitting to his leadership and showing him respect? Husband, does your wife feel the peace, security, and joy that she will when she meets Christ for eternity? Does her union with you make her excited about her union with Christ in eternity? What a challenge! God, give us grace to bring you glory in our marriages! We now turn to the grace and power that God indeed has given us.

Chapter 14:

The Power for Cruciform Love
(1 Thessalonians 4:8-9)

Where does the ability to love in such a selfless way come from? In this book so far, we have been called to a love that cannot come from ourselves! We have said that the primary virtue for new covenant Christians is cruciform love. It is the pattern of giving of self for the good of others. It is a call to selfless living. The call to selflessness is extremely hard!

It is hard because we are sinners, and sin is fundamentally selfishness. It started in the garden. Adam and Eve wanted autonomy (self-rule), and the sons and daughters of Adam have been plagued by the same disease ever since. Isaiah described us as straying sheep. We have all gone astray. We have all turned to our own way. This is why Luther said that since the fall, humanity is "curved in on ourselves." The reality of sinful selfishness is why cruciform love is so difficult.

If our fallen nature is selfish, how can we live selflessly? The short answer is that left to ourselves, we can't, but God is not in the business of leaving his people to themselves. The power for selfless living comes from God. The Holy Spirit empowers us to love *cruciformly*. How though? One of the main ways is by exalting Christ in our hearts. Romans 5 says that we have been justified by faith and have peace with God through our Lord Jesus Christ and that God's love has been poured out into our hearts through the Holy Spirit (Rom. 5:1-5). The Holy Spirit has a "floodlight ministry."

J.I. Packer writes, "When floodlighting is well done, the floodlights are placed so that you do not see them; in fact, you are not supposed to see where the light is coming from; what you are meant to see is just the building on which the floodlights are trained. The intended effect is to make it visible when otherwise it would not be seen for the darkness, and to maximize its dignity by throwing all its details into relief so that you can see it properly. This perfectly illustrated the Spirit's new covenant role. He is, so to speak, the hidden floodlight shining on the Savior. Or think of it this way. It is as if the Spirit stands behind us, throwing light over our shoulder onto Jesus who stands facing us. The Spirit's message to us is never, 'Look at me; listen to me; come to me; get to know me,' but always, 'Look at him, and see his glory; listen to him and hear his word; go to him and have life; get to know him and taste his gift of joy and peace.' The Spirit, we might say, is the matchmaker, the celestial marriage broker, whose role it is to bring us and Christ together and ensure that we stay together."[183] His main ministry is to lift up Jesus and point us to him. In John 16:14, Jesus says, "He will glorify me."

Although many passages could be appealed to, I want to unpack the Spirit's empowerment of cruciform love specifically from 1 Thessalonians 4:8-9. Those verses read, "Therefore whoever disregards this, disregards not man but God, who gives his Holy Spirit to you. Now concerning brotherly love you have no need for anyone to write to you, for you yourselves have been taught by God to love one another." I want to examine a couple of Paul's descriptive statements. Paul's main point in theses verses and the surrounding con-

---

[183] J.I. Packer, *Keep in Step with the Spirit* (Grand Rapids: Baker, 2005), 57-58.

text is the call to holiness. What is fascinating, though, is what Paul writes rather in passing. He describes God as the one who "gives his Holy Spirit" to us. He also describes the believers as being "taught by God."

Promise

Recall the larger story. God had created his people Israel and called them to obey the law. Sadly, they were disobedient right from the start, and it never really got any better. The history of Israel is a history of idolatry and unfaithfulness. God wasn't finished with them, though. Through the prophets, God promised to remake them. He was going to intervene and do something "new." One of the major promises is of a new covenant. Jeremiah 31:31-34 says,

> *Behold, the days are coming, declares the LORD, when I will make a new covenant with the house of Israel and the house of Judah, not like the covenant that I made with their fathers on the day when I took them by the hand to bring them out of the land of Egypt, my covenant that they broke, though I was their husband, declares the LORD. But this is the covenant that I will make with the house of Israel after those days, declares the LORD: I will put my law within them, and I will write it on their hearts. And I will be their God, and they shall be my people. And no longer shall each one teach his neighbor and each his brother, saying, "Know the LORD," for they shall all know me, from the least of them to the greatest, declares the LORD. For I will forgive their iniquity, and I will remember their sin no more.*

Ezekiel also promises this new work of God. In 11:19, we read, "And I will give them one heart, and a new spirit I will put within them. I will remove the heart of stone from their flesh and give them a heart of flesh." Similarly, in Ezekiel 36:25-27, we hear, "I will sprinkle clean water on you, and you shall be clean from all your uncleannesses, and from all your idols I will cleanse you. And I will give you a new heart, and a new spirit I will put within you. And I will remove the heart of stone from your flesh and give you a heart of flesh. And I will put my Spirit within you, and cause you to walk in my statutes and be careful to obey my rules." Ezekiel was probably written about 30 years after Jeremiah, and he is commenting and expanding here on Jeremiah 31. He says that the interiorized law will be the Spirit of God who transforms believers and impels them to free obedience.[184]

Fulfillment

For Paul, as well as for all learned 1st century Jews, Ezekiel 36 and Jeremiah 31 were very important passages.[185] They are two key new covenant passages, and Paul sees these as having been inaugurated in the death and resurrection of Christ and the pouring out of the Spirit at Pentecost. Notice that the tense of the verb "give" is future in Ezekiel 36. When Paul quotes it in 1 Thessalonians, Paul uses a present participle. I want to point out the similarities between the promises given in Ezekiel and what Paul writes here. Note that *didonta* and *dōsō* are from the same verb *didōmi*, meaning "I give:"[186]

1 Thessalonians 4:8—*God, who gives* (didonta) *his Holy Spirit* (to pneuma autou) *to you* (eis hymas).

Ezekiel 11:19—*I will give* (dōsō) *them one heart, and a new spirit* (pneuma) *I will put* (dōsō) *within them* (en autois); *I will remove the heart of stone from their flesh and give them a heart of flesh.*

---

184 Deidun, *New Covenant Morality in Paul*, 37.

185 Ibid., 20, 53.

186 Where these translations differ from the ESV and NIV, they are my own.

Ezekiel 36:26—*And I will give* (dōsō) *you a new heart, and a new spirit* (pneuma) *I will put within you* (en hymin).

Ezekiel 36:27—*And I will put my Spirit within you* (to pneuma mou dōsō en hymin), *and cause you to walk in my statutes and be careful to obey my rules.*

Ezekiel 37:6—*And I will lay sinews upon you, and will cause flesh to come upon you, and cover you with skin, and put breath in you* (dōsō pneuma mou eis hymas), *and you shall live.*

Ezekiel 37:14—*And I will put my Spirit within you* (dōsō to pneuma mou eis hymas), *and you shall live.*[187]

Now notice the similarities between 1 Thessalonians 4:9 and Jeremiah 31 and Isaiah 54:

1 Thessalonians 4:9—*For you yourselves have been taught by God* (theodidaktoi).

Isaiah 54:13—*All your children shall be taught by the LORD* (didaktous theou), *and great shall be the peace of your children.*

Jeremiah 31:34—*And no longer shall each one teach his neighbor and each his brother, saying, "Know the Lord," for they shall all know me, from the least of them to the greatest* (38:34 LXX) (kai ou mē diaxōsin hekastos ton politēn autou... hoti pantes eidēsousin mē).[188]

Notice that what Jeremiah and Isaiah saw as a future has become a present reality for the Thessalonians. They have been taught by God.[189] "Taught by God" probably refers both the teaching of Jesus and the inner working of the Spirit.[190] It is communication from God and a relationship with him.

---

[187] Ibid., 19, 33, 53, 228; Fee, *God's Empowering Presence,* 52.

[188] Peterson, *Possessed by God,* 84.

[189] Ibid., 33.

[190] F.F. Bruce, *1 & 2 Thessalonians,* WBC (Word, 1982), 90.

Cruciform Love

Now we have the Spirit of God, who moves us to follow his decrees and keep his laws. Our old stony heart has been replaced by a fleshly one. We have been taught by God. Notice what Paul says we are taught by God to do: mutual love. This has been an emphasis in 1 Thessalonians (just like it is in every New Testament letter). Consider a sample:

3:6—*"But now that Timothy has come to us from you, and has brought us the good news of your faith and love and reported that you always remember us kindly and long to see us, as we long to see you."*

3:12—*"And may the Lord make you increase and abound in love for one another and for all, as we do for you."*

5:7-8—*"For those who sleep, sleep at night, and those who get drunk, are drunk at night. But since we belong to the day, let us be sober, having put on the breastplate of faith and love, and for a helmet the hope of salvation."*

5:11—*"Therefore encourage one another and build one another up, just as you are doing."*

5:15—*"See that no one repays anyone evil for evil, but always seek to do good to one another and to everyone."*

Love is at the heart of the new covenant call to holiness. It is the Spirit's *principal* work in the life of the believer. It is no wonder that the first fruit of the Spirit listed is *love* (Gal. 5:22f). Love does not come from us. The gospel is the power that transforms us, and the Spirit works in and through us. It is God's activity within the hearts of Christians that impels us to action.[191] God is the one who gives us his Holy Spirit and teaches us to practice cruciform love.

---

[191] Deidun, *New Covenant Morality*, 58.

Chapter 15:

Conclusion

It is my hope and prayer that this book has helped, encouraged, and challenged you. Ethics is an important topic and is worth thinking about. More importantly, it is vital that Christians strive to live in accordance with new covenant ethics. I hope this has given you a foundation to build upon. I also hope Part II has helped you see how central cross-shaped love is for new covenant ethics. As Luke Johnson writes, "The imitation of Christ in his life of service and suffering—not as an act of masochism for the sake of suppressing one's own life but as an act of love for the enhancement of others' lives—is not an optional version of Christian identity. It is the very *essence* of Christian identity. It is the pattern by which every other claim about the spiritual life must be measured if it is to be considered Christian. It is what is learned from Jesus. It is what learning Jesus means."[192] May God give us grace to live such selfless lives. To Him be all the glory!

---

[192] Johnson, *Living Jesus*, 201.

Bibliography

Alcorn, Randy. "Dethroning Money to Treasure Christ Above All." In *For the Fame of God's Name*, edited by Sam Storms and Justin Taylor. Wheaton, IL: Crossway, 2010.

Bahnsen, Greg. *Always Ready*. Nacogdoches, TX: Covenant Media Press, 2006.

_____. *Pushing the Antithesis*. Powder Springs, GA: American Vision, 2007.

Barth, Karl. *Church Dogmatics* IV/2. Edinburgh: T&T Clark International.

Bartholomew, Craig G. and Michael W. Goheen. *The Drama of Scripture*. Grand Rapids: Baker Academic, 2004.

Bloom, Allan. *The Closing of the American Mind*. New York: Simon and Schuster, 1987.

Bock, Darrell L. *Recovering the Real Lost Gospel*. Nashville: B&H Academic, 2010.

Bonhoeffer, Dietrich. *The Cost of Discipleship*. New York: Simon and Schuster, 1995.

_____. *Life Together*. New York: HarperOne, 1954.

Boyd, Gregory A. *The Myth of a Christian Nation*. Grand Rapids: Zondervan, 2005.

_____. *The Myth of a Christian Religion*. Grand Rapids: Zondervan, 2009.

Bruce, F.F. *1 & 2 Thessalonians*. Word Books, 1982.

_____. *Paul: Apostle of the Heart Set Free*. Grand Rapids: Eerdmans, 1997.

Caird, G.B. *Paul's Letters from Prison in the Revised Standard Version*. Oxford: Oxford University Press, 1976.

Camp, Lee. *Mere Discipleship*. Grand Rapids: Brazos Press, 2003.

Claiborne, Shane and Chris Haw. *Jesus for President*. Grand Rapids: Zondervan, 2008.

Cole, Graham A. *He Who Gives Life*. Wheaton, IL: Crossway, 2007.

Conzelmann, Hans. *1 Corinthians*. Philadelphia: Fortress Press, 1975.

Cook, David. *The Moral Maze*. London: SPCK, 1983.

Davis, John Jefferson. *Evangelical Ethics*. Phillipsburg, NJ: P&R, 2004.

Deidun, T.J. *New Covenant Morality in Paul*. Rome: Biblical Institute, 1981.

Dickson, John. *The Best Kept Secret of Christian Mission*. Grand Rapids: Zondervan, 2010.

Dorsey, David A. "The Law of Moses and the Christian: A Compromise." *JETS* 34, no. 3 (September 1991).

Dunn, James G. D. "'The Law of Faith,' 'the Law of the Spirit' and 'the Law of Christ.'" In *Theology and Ethics*, edited by Eugene H. Lovering, Jr. and Jerry L. Sumney. Nashville: Abingdon, 1996.

Fee, Gordon. *The First Epistle to the Corinthians*. New International Commentary on the New Testament. Grand Rapids: Eerdmans, 1987.

_____. *God's Empowering Presence*. Peabody, MA: Hendrick-son, 1994.

Feinberg, John S. and Paul D. Feinberg. *Ethics for a Brave New World*, 2nd edition. Wheaton, IL: Crossway, 2010.

Frame, John. *The Doctrine of the Christian Life*. Phillipsburg, NJ: P&R, 2008.

_____. *The Doctrine of the Knowledge of God*. Phillipsburg, NJ: P&R, 1987.

Furnish, Victor P. *Theology and Ethics in Paul*. Nashville: Abingdon, 1968.

Goheen, Michael W. and Craig G. Bartholomew. *Living at the Crossroads*. Grand Rapids: Baker Academic, 2008.

Gonzales, Justo. *Faith and Wealth*. Eugene, OR: Wipf and Stock, 2002.

Gorman, Michael. *Cruciformity*. Grand Rapids: Eerdmans, 2001.

_____. *Reading Paul*. Eugene, OR: Cascade, 2008.

Hays, Richard B. *The Moral Vision of the New Testament*. New York: HarperOne, 1996.

_____. *1 Corinthians*. Interpretation. Louisville: John Knox Press, 1997.

_____. "Christology and Ethics in Galatians: The Law of Christ." *Catholic Biblical Quarterly* 49, no. 1 (January 1987).

_____. "Crucified with Christ: A Synthesis of the Theology of 1 & 2 Thessalonians, Philemon, Philippians, and Galatians." In *Pauline Theology, Vol. 1*, edited by Jouette M. Bassler. Minneapolis: Fortress Press, 1994.

_____. *Galatians*. The New Interpreter's Bible. Nashville: Abingdon, 2000.

Hill, Michael. *The How and Why of Love*. Australia: Matthias Media, 2002.

Horrell, David G. *Solidarity and Difference*. New York: T&T Clark International, 2005.

Horton, Michael. *Christless Christianity*. Grand Rapids: Baker, 2008.

Jethani, Skye. *The Divine Commodity*. Grand Rapids: Eerdmans, 2009.

Johnson, Luke Timothy. *Living Jesus*. New York: HarperOne, 1999.

Keller, Tim. *The Reason for God*. New York: Dutton, 2008.

Kirk, J.R. Daniel. *Jesus I Have Loved, but Paul?* Grand Rapids: Baker Academic, 2012.

Kreider, Alan and Eleanor Kreider. *Worship and Mission after Christendom*. Scottsdale, PA: Herald Press, 2011.

Lewis, C.S. *The Complete C.S. Lewis*. New York: HarperOne, 2002.

Lindvall, Terry. *Surprised by Laughter*. Nashville: Nelson, 1996.

Longenecker, Richard N. *Galatians*. Dallas: Word, 1990.

Lull, Timothy F., ed. *Martin Luther's Basic Theological Writings*. Minneapolis: Fortress Press, 1989.

Macleod, Donald. *The Person of Christ*. Downers Grove, IL: IVP, 1998.

Mahaney, C.J. *Humility*. Colorado Springs: Multinomah, 2005.

Martyn, J.L. *Galatians*. New York: Doubleday, 1997.

Moo, Douglas J. *The Epistle to the Romans*. The New International Commentary on the New Testament. Grand Rapids: Eerdmans, 1996.

_____. "The Law of Christ as the Fulfillment of the Law of Moses: A Modified Lutheran View." In *Five Views on Law and Gospel*, edited by Stanley N. Gundry. Grand Rapids: Zondervan, 1999.

Morris, Leon. *1 Corinthians*. Tyndale New Testament Commentary. Grand Rapids: Eerdmans, 1985.

Newbigin, Leslie. *The Gospel in a Pluralist Society*. Grand Rapids: Eerdmans, 1989.

O'Brien, Peter T. *The Letter to the Ephesians*. Grand Rapids: Eerdmans, 1999.

Packer, J.I. *Keep in Step With the Spirit*. Grand Rapids: Baker, 2005.

Pearcey, Nancy. *Total Truth*. Wheaton, IL: Crossway, 2005.

Peterson, David. *Possessed by God*. Downers Grove, IL: IVP, 1995.

Piper, John. *This Momentary Marriage*. Wheaton, IL: Crossway, 2009.

Platt, David. *Radical Together*. Colorado Springs: Multinomah, 2011.

Pohl, Christine D. "Hospitality." In *Ancient Faith for the Church's Future*, edited by Mark Husbands and Jeffrey P. Greenman. Downers Grove, IL: IVP Academic, 2008.

Reisinger, John G. *Grace*. Frederick, MD: New Covenant Media, 2008.

Schrage, Wolfgang. *The Ethics of the New Testament*. Philadelphia: Fortress Press, 1982.

Schreiner, Thomas R. *Galatians*. Zondervan Exegetical Commentary. Grand Rapids: Zondervan, 2010.

Sider, Ronald J. *The Scandal of the Evangelical Conscience*. Grand Rapids: Baker, 2005.

Sire, James W. *The Universe Next Door*. Downers Grove, IL: IVP Academic, 2004.

Stinson, Randy and Dan Dumas. *A Guide to Biblical Manhood*. Louisville: The Southern Baptist Theological Seminary, 2011.

Thielman, Frank. *Philippians*. NIV Application Commentary. Grand Rapids: Zondervan, 1995.

Tomlin, Graham. *Spiritual Fitness*. New York: Continuum, 2006.

Tripp, Paul David. *What Did You Expect?* Wheaton, IL: Crossway, 2010.

VanDrunen, David. *BioEthics and the Christian Life*. Wheaton, IL: Crossway, 2009.

Walsh, Brian J. and Richard Middleton. *The Transforming Vision*. Downers Grove, IL: IVP, 1984.

Wells, David. *Losing Our Virtue*. Grand Rapids: Eerdmans, 1998.

White, A. Blake. *What is New Covenant Theology?* Frederick, MD: New Covenant Media, 2012.

White, R.E.O. *Biblical Ethics*. Atlanta: John Knox Press, 1979.

Wilson, Douglas and Christopher Hitchens. *Is Christianity Good for the World?* Moscow, ID: Canon Press, 2008.

Witherington III, Ben. *Conflict and Community in Corinth*. Grand Rapids: Eerdmans, 1995.

_____. *Grace in Galatia*. Grand Rapids: Eerdmans, 1998.

Wolters, Albert M. *Creation Regained*. Grand Rapids: Eerdmans, 2005.

Wright, N.T. *The New Testament and the People of God*. Minneapolis: Fortress, 1992.

_____. *After You Believe*. New York: HarperOne, 2010.

_____. "Faith, Virtue, Justification, and the Journey to Freedom." In *The Word that Leaps the Gap*, edited by J. Ross Wagner, C. Kavin Rowe, and A. Katherine Grieb. Grand Rapids: Eerdmans, 2008.

_____. *Jesus and the Victory of God*. Minneapolis: Fortress, 1996.

_____. *Paul*. Minneapolis: Fortress Press, 2008.

Zaspel, Fred. "Imitating the Incarnation: B.B. Warfield on Following Christ." *Sound of Grace* 183 (Dec 2011-Jan 2012).

Zens, Jon. "This is My Beloved Son, Hear Him." *Searching Together* 25, no. 1-3 (Summer-Winter 1997).

CPSIA information can be obtained at www.ICGtesting.com
Printed in the USA
LVOW12s1939260214

375275LV00019B/805/P